EXPAT GUIDE: CAMBODIA

The essential guide to becoming an expatriate in Cambodia

Disclaimer

General Information Only: The information provided in this book is for general informational purposes only. It should not be considered as professional advice on any subject matter.

No Professional Relationship: Reading this book does not create any professional relationship between the reader and the author or publisher.

Accuracy of Information: While every effort has been made to ensure that the information contained in this book is accurate and up-to-date, the author and publisher make no representations or warranties of any kind, express or implied, about the completeness, accuracy, reliability, suitability, or availability of the content.

Liability Limitation: In no event will the author or publisher be liable for any loss or damage including without limitation, indirect or consequential loss or damage, or any loss or damage whatsoever arising from loss of data or profits arising out of, or in connection with, the use of this book.

External Links: Any links to external websites provided within this book are provided for the reader's convenience only. The author and publisher have no control over the content of these sites and accept no responsibility for them or for any loss or damage that may arise from the reader's use of them.

Professional Advice: The information contained in this book is not intended to replace professional advice. If the reader requires professional advice in relation to any particular matter, he or she should consult an appropriately qualified professional.

Changes to Content: The author and publisher reserve the right to make changes to the content, layout, and other elements of this book without notice.

Contents

Map of Cambodia

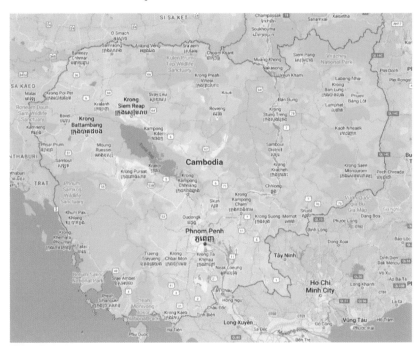

1. Introduction

1.1 Brief Overview of Cambodia

Cambodia, officially known as the Kingdom of Cambodia, is a vibrant country nestled in the southern part of the Indochina Peninsula in Southeast Asia. It is bordered by Thailand to the west and northwest, Laos to the northeast, Vietnam to the east, and the Gulf of Thailand to the southwest.

Cambodia covers a land area of about 181,035 square kilometers and is home to more than 16 million people. The country's landscape is characterized by a central low-lying plain, surrounded by uplands and low mountains. Cambodia is bisected by the Mekong River, one of the world's longest rivers, creating a fertile plain suitable for agriculture, particularly rice cultivation.

Phnom Penh, the capital and largest city, is the political, economic, and cultural center of the country. Other major cities include Siem Reap, Battambang, and Sihanoukville.

Cambodia's history is both rich and turbulent, spanning centuries from the glorious Khmer Empire that built the majestic Angkor Wat, to the dark days of the Khmer Rouge regime. Today, Cambodia is a constitutional monarchy with a multi-party democracy under a monarchy, currently headed by King Norodom Sihamoni.

Its economy is largely agrarian but is rapidly diversifying with growth in sectors such as textiles, construction, garments, and tourism, which is centered around the Angkor Archaeological Park, a UNESCO World Heritage Site. Cambodia also boasts a range of natural attractions, including the Tonlé Sap Lake, mountains, and beautiful tropical islands.

The official language is Khmer, which is spoken by most of the population. Buddhism is the dominant religion, deeply influencing Cambodian culture, art, and everyday life. The culture is rich and varied, with influences from India and China, seen in the country's cuisine, dance, and art.

Despite its challenging past, Cambodia stands today as a country of resilience and charm, offering a unique blend of traditional and modern lifestyles. Cambodia has fascinating history, combined with its natural beauty and the warmth of its people, makes it a compelling destination for expats.

1.2 Why an Expat Guide for Cambodia

Cambodia's unique blend of rich history, diverse cuhavere, vibrant city life, and stunning natural landscapes has increasingly drawn the attention of expatriates from around the world. Whether it's the lure of its burgeoning economy presenting business opportunities, the low cost of living, the allure of its cultural heritage, or the simple desire for an adventure in a land that beautifully marries tradition and modernity, Cambodia is a compelling choice for many seeking to live abroad.

However, while moving to a new country can be an exciting adventure, it's also a complex process that presents its own set of challenges. Every country has unique customs, rules, and cultural nuances that newcomers need to understand and navigate to fully integrate into the society, and Cambodia is no different. Understanding these aspects of life in Cambodia can make the transition smoother and the overall experience more rewarding.

This is where 'Expat Guide: Cambodia' comes in. This guide is designed to provide comprehensive and practical information to current and prospective expatriates considering a move to Cambodia. It delves into various crucial aspects - from understanding the legal process of moving, details on housing and education, insights into the cultural norms and traditions, to offering practical information on healthcare, transportation, and the cost of living.

By shedding light on what you can expect, providing tips on navigating common hurdles, and offering insights on how to immerse yourself in the Cambodian life, we aim to make your move to Cambodia as smooth and rewarding as possible.

Whether you're planning to move for work, retirement, or simply a change of pace, this guide will serve as a comprehensive resource, helping you make informed decisions and better adapt to your new home in the Kingdom of Wonder.

1.3 Myths and Misconceptions about Cambodia

Like many countries, Cambodia is subject to a variety of myths and misconceptions, which can skew the perception of potential expats and visitors. Understanding these myths can help shed light on the real Cambodia that is waiting to be discovered.

Myth 1: Cambodia is Unsafe - While it's true that Cambodia has had a tumultuous history, today's Cambodia is a peaceful and safe country. Like anywhere, certain areas may be safer than others and caution should always be exercised, especially in crowded or less developed areas. However, most visitors and expats living in Cambodia experience a welcoming and secure environment.

Myth 2: Cambodia is Underdeveloped - While it's true that Cambodia is a developing country and certain areas, especially rural ones, lack some of the amenities found in more developed nations, major cities like Phnom Penh and Siem Reap offer a good quality of life with modern conveniences, including high-speed internet, shopping malls, international schools, and advanced healthcare facilities.

Myth 3: English isn't Widely Spoken - Although Khmer is the official language, English is widely spoken, especially in major cities and tourist areas. Many Cambodians, particularly the younger generation and those working in hospitality or business, speak good English.

Myth 4: Cambodia's History is Only About the Khmer Rouge - While the dark period of Khmer Rouge is an undeniable part of Cambodia's history, focusing solely on it overlooks the country's rich and ancient cultural heritage. Cambodia is home to the majestic Angkor Wat, evidence of the powerful Khmer Empire that once ruled much of Southeast Asia.

Myth 5: Cambodian Cuisine is Less Varied than its Neighbors - While Thai and Vietnamese cuisines are well-known worldwide, Cambodian, or Khmer, cuisine doesn't get the recognition it deserves. Khmer food is a delightful mix of flavors, with unique dishes such as Amok and Kampot pepper crab.

As we journey through this guide, we will continue to dispel any misconceptions and offer a well-rounded view of life in Cambodia, helping you fully understand and appreciate the intricacies of this fascinating country.

2. Understanding Expat Life

2.1 What is an Expat?

Expat, short for expatriate, is a term used to describe a person who resides in a country different from their country of birth or citizenship. The reasons for choosing an expat life are varied and individual - some people become expats for job opportunities, while others may move for a better quality of life, to experience a new culture, for education, or even to retire.

Being an expat goes beyond just living in a new country. It involves embracing a different culture, learning new ways of life, and often, navigating through a foreign language. It can be an enriching and transformative experience, offering a new perspective on life and the world. At the same time, expat life can come with its own set of challenges, including homesickness, cultural shock, and the task of building a new social network.

It's important to note that the term 'expat' doesn't usually refer to all immigrants. It's typically used to describe those who plan to live temporarily in a foreign country or have a certain level of privilege, often associated with their job type, income, or nationality. The distinction between who is considered an 'expat' and who is an 'immigrant' can be complex and contentious, and perceptions can vary depending on different contexts.

In this guide, we use the term 'expat' to refer to anyone from any country who is considering moving to or is currently living in Cambodia, regardless of their reasons for relocating or the duration of their stay.

2.2 The Expat Journey: Stages and Transitions

The journey of an expat often follows a series of stages, each with its unique characteristics, opportunities, and challenges. Understanding these stages can help you navigate expat life more effectively.

Stage 1: Research and Decision Making - This stage involves exploring potential destinations, researching the local culture, legal procedures, cost of living, and any other relevant factors. It's also the time when you make the critical decision to make the move.

Stage 2: Preparation and Relocation - Once the decision is made, this stage involves logistical preparations, including securing a visa, finding accommodation, booking flights, and packing. This phase can be both exciting and stressful as the moving day approaches.

Stage 3: The Honeymoon Phase - Upon arrival in the new country, many expats experience a honeymoon phase where everything in the new environment seems exciting and exotic. This phase is characterized by exploration and fascination with the local culture, people, and places.

Stage 4: Culture Shock - As the initial excitement wears off, the reality of the differences between one's home country and the new one sets in. This can lead to a period of culture shock, where expats may feel disoriented, confused, or frustrated as they navigate cultural differences and overcome language barriers.

Stage 5: Adjustment - This stage sees expats slowly getting accustomed to their new surroundings. They start understanding the local customs and traditions, making new friends, and feeling more comfortable navigating their day-to-day life.

Stage 6: Adaptation or Acceptance - This is the stage of full acceptance or adaptation to the new culture. Expats feel at home in the new country, having created a new routine and established a social network. It doesn't mean they fully assimilate or lose their own cultural identity, but rather they learn to appreciate and live comfortably within the new culture. Each expat's journey is unique, and these stages may not always follow a linear path. It's common to move back and forth between these stages or experience them in a different order. The duration of each stage can also vary greatly depending on the individual's personal circumstances and coping skills. Understanding these stages can help expats prepare for, recognize, and manage these transitions more effectively.

2.3 Benefits and Challenges of Being an Expat

Living as an expat comes with its own set of benefits and challenges. Understanding these can help you make an informed decision and prepare for the journey ahead.

Benefits of Being an Expat:

- **Personal Growth** - Living in a new country pushes you out of your comfort zone, offering opportunities for personal growth. You develop new skills, learn a new language, and gain a deeper understanding of the world.
- **Cultural Experience** - As an expat, you get the opportunity to immerse yourself in a new culture. This includes trying new foods, celebrating local festivals, and adopting new customs and traditions.
- **Career Opportunities** - Many expats find better job opportunities abroad. Some companies even offer incentives for employees to work overseas, such as paid housing or a higher salary.
- **Improved Quality of Life** - Depending on where you move, you might find that you enjoy a better quality of life. This could be due to a lower cost of living, better weather, or more leisure opportunities.

Challenges of Being an Expat:

- **Culture Shock** - Adapting to a new culture can be challenging. You may struggle with language barriers, different social norms, or unfamiliar food.
- Homesickness - It's common for expats to miss home. This can include missing family and friends, familiar places, or comforts from home.
- Administrative Hurdles - Living in a new country comes with its fair share of red tape. You'll likely have to navigate through unfamiliar immigration procedures, housing contracts, and local laws.
- Adapting to New Social Norms - Understanding and adapting to the social norms of a new country can be challenging but crucial for integration. Misunderstanding these norms can lead to unintentional offense or social faux pas.

Being aware of these benefits and challenges will allow you to better prepare for life as an expat. Remember, it's entirely normal to experience ups and downs along the way. The key lies in staying open-minded, adaptable, and patient as you navigate through this exciting journey of living abroad.

3. Why Choose Cambodia?

3.1 Geography and Climate

Cambodia, officially known as the Kingdom of Cambodia, is in Southeast Asia, bordered by Thailand to the northwest, Laos to the northeast, and Vietnam to the east, with the Gulf of Thailand to its southwest. Covering an area of approximately 181,035 square kilometers, Cambodia offers a diverse range of geographical features that include mountains, plains, and a stunning coastline.

Geographical Features:

- **Mountains** - The Cardamom Mountains and the Dangrek Range are two significant mountain ranges in

Cambodia. The Cardamom Mountains are home to many endangered species and form one of the largest unfragmented forest landscapes in Southeast Asia.

- **Plains** - The Central Plains represent the agricultural heartland of Cambodia and include the Tonle Sap basin and the lower reaches of the Mekong River. This area is home to Cambodia's fertile rice paddies, which contribute significantly to the country's agricultural production.
- **Coastline** - The southwestern part of the country features a 443-kilometer-long coastline along the Gulf of Thailand, dotted with picturesque fishing villages and several pristine islands.

Climate:

Cambodia has a tropical monsoon climate, characterized by a wet and a dry season. The average temperature is about 27 degrees Celsius (80.6 degrees Fahrenheit), although it can get cooler in the mountains.

Wet Season - The wet season (May to October) is characterized by high humidity and heavy rainfall due to the southwest monsoon. Rain showers typically occur in the late afternoon or evening, turning the countryside into a lush green landscape.

Dry Season - The dry season (November to April) is characterized by low rainfall and is divided into the cool season (November to February) and the hot season (March to May). The cool season, with comfortable temperatures and minimal rainfall, is generally the most popular time to visit.

Understanding Cambodia's geography and climate can greatly enhance your experience as an expat, as these factors can influence everything from travel plans to what kind of housing or clothing you might need.

3.2 Culture and Heritage

Cambodia's culture is deeply rooted in its history, with influences from Indian and Chinese civilizations, as well as neighboring Southeast Asian cultures. The country's rich cultural heritage is reflected in its arts, architecture, cuisine, music, and customs.

Religion: Buddhism is the dominant religion, practiced by approximately 95% of the population. The Cambodian variant of Theravada Buddhism permeates many aspects of daily life, from architecture to the arts and social norms. Respect for religious customs is important, particularly when visiting temples or during religious festivals.

Arts and Architecture: Cambodia is globally renowned for its ancient architecture, most notably the Angkor Wat, a magnificent temple complex and the largest religious monument in the world. Khmer architecture, which includes temples, irrigation systems, and cities, is a source of national pride. The arts scene is also vibrant, with traditional arts such as shadow puppetry, silk weaving, and Apsara dance thriving alongside modern forms of expression.

Language: The official language is Khmer, spoken by most of the population. While English is increasingly understood, particularly in urban areas and among younger generations, learning some basic Khmer phrases can go a long way in connecting with local people.

Social Etiquette: Cambodian society values harmony and non-confrontation. Politeness, respect for elders, and humility are important cultural norms. The traditional greeting or 'sampeah' involves pressing the palms together in a prayer-like gesture and is often accompanied by a bow. The height of the hands and depth of the bow depend on the status of the person you are greeting.

Cuisine: Cambodian cuisine is a tantalizing blend of flavors, drawing influences from Chinese, Indian, and Thai cooking. Rice is a staple, and fish from the Mekong and Tonle Sap rivers feature prominently in many dishes. The national dish, Amok, is a coconut milk curry typically cooked with fish. Understanding and appreciating Cambodia's cultural heritage is not only a fascinating journey but also essential for a smooth transition to life in Cambodia. As an expat, respecting local customs and participating in cultural practices can foster a deeper connection with the Cambodian people and your new surroundings.

3.3 Cost of Living

One of the major attractions for expats considering a move to Cambodia is the low cost of living. However, costs can vary depending on your lifestyle, location, and personal preferences.

Housing: Housing costs in Cambodia are generally affordable, especially compared to Western standards. Rental prices can vary widely based on location, size, and amenities. For instance, in Phnom Penh, a one-bedroom apartment in the city center might cost around $500-$600 per month, while outside the city center, the price can drop to around $200-$300. Prices tend to be lower in smaller towns and rural areas.

Food: Eating in Cambodia can be very affordable, especially if you enjoy local cuisine. A meal at a local restaurant might cost just a few dollars, while a three-course meal at a mid-range restaurant can be around $15-$20. Groceries are also reasonably priced, particularly fresh produce at local markets.

Transportation: Public transportation is limited in Cambodia, but there are various inexpensive alternatives such as tuk-tuks, moto-taxis, and bicycles. Buying a used car can be relatively expensive due to high import taxes, but motorbikes are a popular and cost-effective option.

Utilities and Internet: Basic utilities for a one-bedroom apartment, including electricity, cooling, water, and garbage, might cost around $50-$100 per month. The Internet is reasonably priced, with unlimited broadband data plans available for around $15-$20 per month.

Healthcare: Private healthcare in Cambodia can be costly, especially for serious or complex treatments which may require evacuation to neighboring Thailand or Singapore. It is recommended for expats to have comprehensive health insurance to cover these potential expenses.

Leisure and Entertainment: Costs for leisure and entertainment activities can vary widely. Entrance to museums and historical sites is typically inexpensive, and local events or festivals are often free. Western-style entertainment, like dining in upscale restaurants, attending live shows, or visiting international-standard gyms, can be more costly.

Keep in mind that while the cost of living can be lower in Cambodia, it's important to budget for unexpected costs or emergencies. Your cost of living will depend largely on your lifestyle and personal choices.

3.4 Safety and Security Considerations

Understanding safety and security considerations is an essential part of living in any foreign country. While Cambodia is generally regarded as safe for expats, there are certain issues that you should be aware of.

Crime: Petty crime such as bag-snatching, pickpocketing, and smartphone theft is common, particularly in tourist areas and in the capital city, Phnom Penh. It's advisable to remain vigilant, avoid flashing expensive items, and keep your belongings secure. Violent crime against foreigners is relatively rare but can occur, especially in isolated areas or late at night.

Traffic Safety: Road conditions and traffic safety can be major concerns in Cambodia. Traffic rules are not always followed, and accidents are common. If you plan to drive, particularly a motorbike, ensure you are confident, cautious, and always wear a helmet. Avoid driving at night if possible due to poor lighting and the increased risk of accidents.

Health Risks: Medical facilities in Cambodia are limited, particularly outside of Phnom Penh. Make sure to have comprehensive travel insurance that includes evacuation coverage in case of serious illness or injury. Be mindful of food and water hygiene to avoid common illnesses such as traveler's diarrhea.

Natural Disasters: Cambodia is prone to seasonal monsoons, which can cause flooding and landslides, particularly in rural areas. Tropical storms and typhoons can also occur. Familiarize yourself with local disaster plans and stay informed about weather warnings.

Scams: Like many tourist destinations, scams can be an issue. Common scams involve inflated prices, counterfeit goods, and rigged meters in taxis or tuk-tuks. Always negotiate prices in advance and be wary of deals that seem too good to be true.

Landmines: While the situation has improved significantly, unexploded ordnance from past conflicts still poses a risk in some rural areas. Stick to well-trodden paths, particularly when visiting remote temple sites or hiking.

While these safety considerations may sound concerning, it's important to remember that many expats live in Cambodia without any issues. By staying informed, taking precautions, and using common sense, you can safely enjoy everything Cambodia has to offer.

3.5 Political and Socioeconomic Climate

Cambodia's political and socioeconomic climate is an important aspect to consider when planning to live there as an expat.

Political Climate: Cambodia is a constitutional monarchy with a multiparty democracy under a monarchy. The King is the head of state, while the Prime Minister is the head of government. The political scene is largely dominated by the Cambodian People's Party, which has been in power for several decades. The political environment has been relatively stable, although there have been periods of tension and political disputes.

Human Rights and Freedom of Speech: International observers have raised concerns about issues such as human rights, freedom of speech, and media freedom in Cambodia. While these issues might not directly affect your daily life as an expat, they are worth being aware of to understand the broader context of the country you are living in.

Economic Climate: Cambodia's economy has been one of the fastest growing in Asia, with tourism, agriculture, and garments as the main economic pillars. However, it remains a developing country with significant challenges, including poverty and income inequality.

Currency: The official currency is the Cambodian Riel, but the US dollar is widely used in everyday transactions, especially in urban areas and for larger purchases. ATMs often dispense US dollars, and change might be given in a combination of dollars and riel.

Development: In recent years, Cambodia has seen significant development, especially in major cities like Phnom Penh and Siem Reap. Infrastructure has been improving, with investments in roads, bridges, and buildings. Internet access and mobile connectivity have also significantly improved.

Understanding the political and socioeconomic climate of Cambodia will provide a broader context for your experiences as an expat. It can shape everything from job opportunities to the cost of living and influence your overall perception of life in the country.

3.6 Comparisons with Other Popular Expat Destinations

When considering Cambodia as a potential home, it can be helpful to compare it with other popular expat destinations in terms of living conditions, opportunities, and lifestyle.

Thailand: As Cambodia's western neighbor, Thailand is often the most immediate comparison. Thailand has a more developed infrastructure, particularly in terms of healthcare and transportation. It is also known for its bustling cities and beautiful beaches. However, the cost of living in Cambodia is generally lower, and the visa process can be less complicated.

Vietnam: To the east, Vietnam offers a dynamic blend of traditional culture and modern growth. It has a vibrant economy and is known for its street food, natural beauty, and bustling cities like Ho Chi Minh City and Hanoi. However, the pace of life in Vietnam can be faster and more chaotic compared to Cambodia. Additionally, while English is commonly spoken in the business environment in Vietnam, Cambodians' proficiency in English has been growing, making it easier for expats to communicate.

Malaysia: Malaysia is another popular expat destination in Southeast Asia, known for its multicultural society, stable economy, and high standard of living. Its capital, Kuala

Lumpur, is a modern city with a range of international amenities. However, Malaysia can be more expensive than Cambodia, and it presents a different cultural experience.

Indonesia (Bali): Bali, Indonesia, is popular with expats for its tropical climate, natural beauty, and spiritual culture. It has a strong community of digital nomads and entrepreneurs. However, the cost of living can be higher, particularly in popular areas like Ubud and Seminyak.

Philippines: The Philippines offers beautiful beaches, English-speaking locals, and a low cost of living. However, the country faces issues with traffic congestion, especially in Manila, and its infrastructure is not as developed.

Ultimately, choosing an expat destination is a highly personal decision, depending on your lifestyle preferences, work opportunities, and desired cultural experiences. Each country has its own unique offerings, and Cambodia's blend of affordability, cultural richness, and friendly locals make it a compelling choice for many expats.

3.7 Ecological Diversity and Outdoor Activities

Cambodia offers a wide range of natural beauty and outdoor activities, making it an appealing destination for expats who enjoy nature and adventure.

Natural Landscapes: Cambodia's landscapes range from the rugged mountains in the north to the low-lying central plains to the beautiful coastline along the Gulf of Thailand. This diversity makes it perfect for outdoor enthusiasts interested in everything from hiking to beach combing.

Biodiversity: The country is rich in biodiversity, with several national parks and wildlife sanctuaries, such as the Virachey National Park and the Cardamom Mountains. These areas offer the chance to see an array of wildlife, including elephants, gibbons, and a variety of bird species.

Outdoor Activities: For the adventurous, there are plenty of opportunities for trekking, mountain biking, rock climbing, and kayaking. In addition, Cambodia's coastline and offshore islands offer beautiful spots for snorkeling, diving, and fishing.

The Mekong River: This iconic river flows through Cambodia, providing opportunities for boat tours, fishing, and birdwatching. It's also home to the critically endangered Irrawaddy dolphin, which can be spotted in the waters near Kratie.

Angkor Archaeological Park: While not strictly natural, the ruins of Angkor are often intertwined with the surrounding jungle, giving a unique blend of cultural and natural exploration. Sunrise and sunset visits offer especially stunning views.

However, it's important to note that while exploring Cambodia's beautiful outdoors, it's essential to respect the environment and contribute to conservation efforts. Be mindful of your waste, stay on designated paths, avoid disturbing wildlife, and consider supporting eco-tours or conservation organizations.

With its varied ecosystems and stunning landscapes, Cambodia provides a captivating setting for expats who appreciate the outdoors and wish to explore the country's natural wonders.

3.8 Growing Expat-Friendly Services and Amenities

As Cambodia continues to welcome more expats and international visitors, the country has also seen significant growth in services and amenities catering specifically to this diverse community. Here are a few examples:

International Cuisine: While traditional Khmer cuisine is a must-try, expats can also find a wide variety of international food options in Cambodia, particularly in larger cities like Phnom Penh and Siem Reap. From Italian pasta to American-style burgers, Japanese sushi, and Indian curries, your cravings for global flavors will not be disappointed.

Medical Facilities: There's been a noticeable improvement in medical facilities targeting expats, with the establishment of international clinics and hospitals. These institutions often have English-speaking staff and offer a standard of care that is more in line with what expats might be accustomed to in their home countries.

International Schools: The number of international schools in Cambodia has increased, providing diverse and globally recognized curricula. This growth is especially beneficial for expat families concerned about providing quality education for their children.

Expat Communities and Social Events: Various social events, clubs, and organizations cater to the expat community in Cambodia. These can be great resources for networking, making friends, and feeling more at home in your new environment.

Shopping Malls and Supermarkets: Modern shopping malls and supermarkets offering a range of international goods and brands have become more common in major cities, making it easier to find familiar products from home.

While Cambodia still retains its unique culture and charm, these growing expat-friendly services and amenities can make the transition to living in Cambodia more comfortable and enjoyable for foreigners.

4. Legal Considerations

4.1 Visa Types and Application Process

When planning to move to Cambodia, understanding the different visa types and the application process is critical. Cambodia's visa policy is relatively straightforward, and there are several options available depending on your purpose and duration of stay:

Tourist Visa (T): This is suitable for short visits and allows you to stay in Cambodia for 30 days. It can be obtained upon arrival at the airport or at certain land border crossings, but it is advisable to get it in advance through the e-visa online service. Please note that a Tourist Visa can be extended only once for an additional 30 days.

Ordinary Visa (E): Also known as a business visa, the Ordinary Visa is a better choice for those planning to stay long term. Initially, it allows a stay of up to 30 days but can be extended for one month, three months, six months, or one year. Unlike the Tourist Visa, the Ordinary Visa can be extended indefinitely.

Retirement Visa (ER): If you are over 55 and do not plan to work in Cambodia, you can apply for a Retirement Visa. This visa is initially valid for one year and can be renewed annually. To qualify, you must show proof of retirement and financial solvency.

Work Visa (EG): This is for those who intend to work in Cambodia. To get this visa, you will need to have a job offer from a Cambodian company. The company will typically handle the work visa process.

The application process for a Cambodian visa typically requires the following documents: a passport valid for at least six months from the entry date, a completed visa application form, one recent passport-sized photograph, and the visa fee. You can apply for a visa on arrival, but many prefer to apply for an e-visa online to avoid potential queues or complications at the airport.

Please note that visa requirements and policies can change, so it is advisable to check the latest information from the Cambodian Embassy or consulate in your home country before your departure.

4.2 Work Permits

For expats planning to work in Cambodia, it's crucial to understand the process of obtaining a work permit. Here is a basic rundown of the process:

Eligibility: Expats who possess an Ordinary Visa (E) and are employed in Cambodia are eligible for a work permit. This includes both full-time and part-time work.

Application Process: The employer usually takes care of the work permit application process. This involves applying to the Ministry of Labor and Vocational Training, along with required documents including the employment contract, a health certificate, passport photos, and copies of the employee's passport and visa.

Annual Renewal: Work permits must be renewed annually. The process should begin in January and be completed by the end of March. Fines may be applied for late renewals.

Work Permit Card: Upon approval of the work permit, you will receive a work permit card. This card should be kept safe and presented when requested by the authorities.

Changes to Employment: If you change your employer while in Cambodia, your new employer must apply for a new work permit for you. Similarly, if you leave your job, your work permit will no longer be valid, and you will need to apply for an appropriate visa or permit to maintain your legal status in Cambodia.

It's important to remember that working in Cambodia without a valid work permit can lead to fines and other penalties. Always ensure that you are legally authorized to work in Cambodia. It's also advisable to check the most current regulations, as immigration and labor laws can change.

(Note: The laws regarding work permits are subject to change. Always consult the latest resources or a legal professional for the most accurate information.)

4.3 Renewal and Long-term Stay Considerations

Staying long-term in Cambodia requires a clear understanding of visa renewals and the regulations around them. Here are some key considerations:

Ordinary Visa (E) Renewals: As previously mentioned, the Ordinary Visa (E) can be extended for one month, three months, six months, or one year. Unlike the Tourist Visa, the Ordinary Visa can be extended indefinitely. Visa extensions can be arranged through travel agencies, visa agents, or the Cambodian Immigration Department.

Validity of Visas: It's important to note that a visa becomes invalid if you leave Cambodia (unless you have a multiple-entry visa), and you'll need to obtain a new one upon re-entry. A multiple-entry visa allows you to leave and re-enter multiple times during the validity period of your visa.

Overstay Penalties: Overstaying your visa can lead to serious consequences, including fines and potential bans from re-entry into Cambodia. Therefore, it's essential to keep track of your visa expiration date and renew it in a timely manner.

Retirement Visa (ER): For retirees, the Retirement Visa (ER) offers a simple path to long-term stay. This visa is initially valid for one year and can be renewed annually. However, it does require proof of retirement and financial solvency.

Long-term Stay Perks: Long-term stay in Cambodia offers several benefits including access to local pricing for many goods and services, potential tax benefits, and the ability to immerse oneself fully in the local culture and community. Always keep yourself updated with the latest visa regulations by checking with the Cambodian Embassy or consulate in your home country. It's also a good idea to seek advice from a legal professional or a visa agency, especially when planning for a long-term stay in Cambodia.

(Note: Visa regulations can change. Always consult the latest resources or a legal professional for the most accurate information.)

4.4 Requirements for Permanent Residency and Citizenship

Acquiring permanent residency or citizenship in Cambodia involves a different set of procedures and requirements. Here is the general process:

Permanent Residency: Cambodia does not offer a permanent residency program in the same way many Western countries do. Long-term expats typically continue to renew their Ordinary Visa (E), which can be extended indefinitely.

Citizenship: Acquiring Cambodian citizenship is possible, but the process is complicated and time-consuming. It generally involves residing in the country for a minimum of seven years, having a solid command of the Khmer language, and demonstrating good character and a genuine commitment to the Cambodian way of life.

Citizenship through Investment: The Cambodian government has a program whereby foreigners can acquire citizenship through a significant economic investment in the country. The details and requirements of this program can change, so it is important to contact the Cambodian embassy or consulate in your home country for the most current information.

Dual Citizenship: Cambodia allows dual citizenship. Therefore, if a foreigner becomes a Cambodian citizen, they are not required to renounce their original nationality. However, it's essential to check the laws of your home country, as not all countries permit dual citizenship.

In any case, seeking permanent residency or citizenship is a major decision and involves many legalities. It's recommended to seek the counsel of a legal professional to fully understand the implications and requirements.

Please remember that immigration laws are subject to change. Always consult the latest resources or a legal professional for the most accurate information.

4.5 Legal Rights and Responsibilities

Understanding your legal rights and responsibilities is crucial when living in a foreign country. In Cambodia, as an expat, you should be aware of the following:

Respect for Local Laws: As a foreign resident, you are subject to Cambodian laws. This includes everything from traffic laws to regulations about public behavior. It's important to familiarize yourself with local customs and legal expectations.

Property Ownership: Cambodia has specific laws regarding property ownership by foreigners. While foreigners can own apartments and condominium units outright (if the property is not on the ground floor), they are generally prohibited from owning land.

Employment Laws: If you're working in Cambodia, be aware of your rights and responsibilities as outlined in the Cambodian Labor Law. This includes understanding the terms of your employment contract, knowing the legal working hours, and being aware of your rights in case of disputes.

Tax Obligations: As a resident in Cambodia, you are likely subject to local taxes on your income. If you're working, your employer will typically handle income tax withholding. However, it's crucial to understand your tax obligations, especially if you have income from sources outside of your employment.

Legal Protection: In terms of legal protection, it's important to note that while Cambodia's legal system is improving, it can be quite different from what you might be used to in your home country. The court proceedings are typically conducted in the Khmer language, and legal representation may be necessary in case of legal disputes.

It's recommended to seek the advice of a local legal professional to understand fully your legal rights and obligations as an expat in Cambodia.

Please remember that legal frameworks can change. Always consult the latest resources or a legal professional for the most accurate information.

4.6 Laws Specific to Foreigners

While living in Cambodia, it's important to be aware of certain laws that apply specifically to foreigners. Some of these laws include:

Visa Regulations: As discussed earlier, adhering to the terms of your visa is essential. Overstaying your visa or working without a work permit can result in fines and deportation.

Property Ownership Laws: Foreigners can own property in Cambodia, but with certain restrictions. Foreigners can own apartments and condominiums if the property is not on the ground floor, but they cannot own land directly.

Driving Laws: Foreigners are required to have a Cambodian driver's license to drive in Cambodia. While an International Driving Permit (IDP) may be used for a short period, you should obtain a local license for long-term stay.

Work Permits: If you're working in Cambodia, you need a work permit. Working without a valid work permit is considered illegal and can result in penalties.

Exit Taxes: When leaving Cambodia, foreigners are required to pay an exit tax. This is typically included in your airline ticket cost, but it's good to confirm this with your airline.

These are just a few examples. Laws can vary depending on specific situations, and new laws may be introduced. It's crucial to stay updated and seek professional advice if you're unsure about anything.

Please remember that the laws are subject to change. Always consult the latest resources or a legal professional for the most accurate information.

4.7 Dealing with Legal Disputes

Despite our best intentions, legal disputes can sometimes occur. If you find yourself in a legal dispute in Cambodia, here are some important things to consider:

Legal Representation: You have the right to hire a lawyer to represent you in any legal disputes. It's advisable to choose a lawyer who is familiar with the Cambodian legal system and preferably one who can communicate in your native language.

Language Barrier: Legal proceedings are conducted in Khmer. If you don't speak the language, it's essential to have an interpreter present.

Dispute Resolution: Mediation and arbitration services are available in Cambodia and can be an efficient way to resolve disputes without resorting to court proceedings. This is particularly relevant in business and commercial disputes.

Respecting Local Laws: It's important to always show respect for the local laws, customs, and traditions. Demonstrating respect can go a long way in resolving any issues you may face.

Legal Aid: In certain circumstances, you may be eligible for legal aid. Non-profit organizations and international agencies provide such services, particularly for issues related to human rights and labor disputes.

Contacting Your Embassy: In case of serious legal issues, including criminal charges, it's crucial to contact your embassy as soon as possible. They can provide a list of recommended lawyers, and while they cannot intervene directly with the Cambodian legal system, they can ensure you are treated fairly under Cambodian law.

While this guide provides an overview, it's always advisable to consult a legal professional when dealing with legal disputes in Cambodia.

Please remember that legal procedures can change. Always consult the latest resources or a legal professional for the most accurate information.

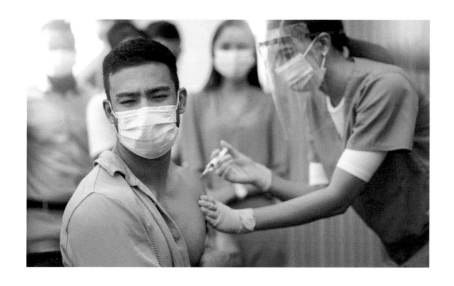

5. Health and Insurance

5.1 Healthcare System in Cambodia

The healthcare system in Cambodia has seen significant improvement over the years, but it is still developing and may not be on par with Western standards. Here are the key points to understand:

Public Healthcare: The public healthcare system in Cambodia is funded by the government and international donors. While efforts are being made to improve it, public healthcare facilities, particularly in rural areas, often lack resources and may not meet the expectations of most expats.

Private Healthcare: In urban areas such as Phnom Penh and Siem Reap, private clinics and hospitals offer a higher standard of care with English-speaking staff. These facilities typically cater to foreigners and the Cambodian middle class. However, the cost of treatment at private facilities can be considerably higher than at public hospitals.

Specialized Treatment: For complex medical conditions and emergencies, medical evacuation to a nearby country with superior medical facilities, like Thailand or Singapore, may be necessary. It's essential to have a health insurance plan that covers such scenarios.

Pharmacies: Pharmacies are widespread in Cambodia, and many medications can be purchased without a prescription. However, the quality of medications can vary, and counterfeit medications have been reported. It's recommended to stick to reputable pharmacies and, when possible, bring a sufficient supply of prescription medications from home.

Preventive Measures: Vaccinations, good hygiene practices, and preventive measures against diseases common in Cambodia, such as dengue fever and malaria, are essential. When considering healthcare in Cambodia, it's crucial to have comprehensive health insurance coverage that suits your specific needs and includes medical evacuation coverage if necessary.

Please remember that healthcare services and standards can change. Always consult the latest resources or a healthcare professional for the most accurate information.

5.2 Health Insurance Options

A comprehensive to healthcare coverage in Cambodia, having a comprehensive insurance plan is crucial. Here are some insurance options to consider:

International Health Insurance: Many expats choose international health insurance plans, which typically provide comprehensive coverage, including options for outpatient care, dental and eye care, maternity coverage, and medical evacuation. These plans also have the advantage of being portable if you move to another country.

Local Health Insurance: Some local Cambodian insurance companies offer health insurance plans. While these plans may be cheaper, they often offer less comprehensive coverage, and customer service may not be available in English. Also, they typically do not cover medical treatment outside Cambodia.

Travel Insurance: Short-term visitors often rely on travel insurance plans, which can include some health coverage. However, these plans are not suitable for long-term residents, as they typically only cover emergencies and not regular health check-ups or chronic conditions.

Employer-Sponsored Insurance: If you're moving to Cambodia for work, your employer may provide health insurance as part of your benefits package. Be sure to check exactly what is covered under these plans, as the level of coverage can vary widely.

When choosing a health insurance plan, it's important to consider your personal health needs, budget, and the type of coverage provided. For example, if you have a pre-existing condition, ensure it's covered by the plan. Also, check whether the plan provides coverage for medical evacuation, which may be necessary for serious medical conditions given the state of healthcare in some parts of Cambodia.

Please remember that health insurance options and services can change. Always consult the latest resources or a healthcare professional for the most accurate information.

5.3 Vaccinations and Preventive Care

When planning your move to Cambodia, it's essential to take certain preventive health measures to protect yourself from diseases. Here are some steps you can take:

Routine Vaccinations: Ensure that your routine vaccinations are up to date. These may include vaccines for measles, mumps, rubella (MMR), diphtheria, tetanus, pertussis (DTaP), varicella (chickenpox), polio, and your yearly flu shot.

Travel Vaccinations: Depending on your specific circumstances, the following vaccinations are typically recommended for travel to Cambodia: Hepatitis A, Hepatitis B, Typhoid, Japanese Encephalitis, Rabies, and Yellow Fever (only for travelers coming from a country where Yellow Fever is present).

Malaria Prophylaxis: Malaria is present in some parts of Cambodia, and preventive medication may be recommended if you plan to visit or live in these areas. Consult your healthcare provider for advice tailored to your specific situation.

Dengue Fever: There's no vaccine for dengue fever, which is common in Cambodia. Prevention involves protecting yourself from mosquito bites, particularly during the day when dengue-carrying mosquitoes are most active.

Health Checks: Regular health checks and screenings can help identify potential health issues early and ensure you remain in good health. This is especially important in a country like Cambodia where healthcare services may not be as advanced as in Western countries.

Remember, your personal health needs will determine which vaccinations and preventive measures you should take. Always consult with a healthcare provider, ideally one with experience in travel medicine, before moving to Cambodia. Please note that health advice can change. Always consult the latest resources or a healthcare professional for the most accurate information.

5.4 Dealing with Medical Emergencies

Knowing what to do in a medical emergency in Cambodia can be lifesaving. Here's an outline of some key points to remember:

Emergency Numbers: Cambodia does not have a universal emergency number like 911 in the U.S. Instead, different services have different numbers. You can call 119 for ambulance and fire emergencies, and 118 for police. Some private hospitals have their own emergency numbers, which you should have if you're staying near one of these facilities.

Immediate Care: In case of a medical emergency, you will likely be taken to the nearest hospital. In major cities like Phnom Penh and Siem Reap, private hospitals typically offer a better standard of emergency care than public hospitals.

Medical Evacuation: If you suffer a severe illness or injury, you may need to be medically evacuated to a nearby country with superior healthcare facilities, such as Thailand or Singapore. Ensure your health insurance covers medical evacuation.

Pharmacies: For minor ailments, local pharmacies can help. However, bear in mind that the level of English spoken may vary, and counterfeit medications have been reported.

First Aid Training: Having basic first aid training can be incredibly valuable in a medical emergency, especially if you plan to travel to more remote areas of Cambodia.

It's worth noting that medical emergency response times in Cambodia may not be as quick as in your home country, particularly outside major cities. Therefore, taking preventive measures to avoid illness or injury is particularly important. Please remember that emergency services and healthcare standards can change. Always consult the latest resources or a healthcare professional for the most accurate information.

5.5 Mental Health Resources

Moving to a new country can be challenging and, at times, stressful. It's important to take care of not just your physical health but also your mental health. Here are some resources and tips for maintaining mental well-being while living in Cambodia:

Therapy and Counseling Services: A few therapists and counselors operate in Cambodia, particularly in major cities. These professionals can provide support for a variety of mental health concerns, from anxiety and depression to adjustment issues. Services are available in English and other languages.

Online Services: If you prefer or require mental health support from your home country, consider online therapy or telehealth services. Many therapists now offer services over the internet, which can be particularly useful for expats.

Support Groups: There are various expat support groups in Cambodia where you can connect with others who might be experiencing similar challenges. These communities can provide valuable advice, empathy, and camaraderie.

Self-Care: Regular exercise, a healthy diet, staying connected with loved ones, and taking time to relax and do things you enjoy are all essential for maintaining good mental health.

Emergency Support: If you or someone you know is in crisis, seek immediate help. Contact your nearest hospital or your country's consulate or embassy, who can help direct you to appropriate resources.

Please remember that mental health is as important as physical health and it's okay to seek help if you're feeling stressed, anxious, depressed, or struggling in any way.

Please remember that mental health resources and services can change. Always consult the latest resources or a mental health professional for the most accurate information.

6. Housing and Accommodation

6.1 Renting vs. Buying

When relocating to Cambodia, one of the first decisions you'll need to make is whether to rent or buy property. Here are some factors to consider:

Renting in Cambodia:

Ease and Flexibility: Renting can provide a great deal of flexibility, making it a popular choice among expats who are unsure about their long-term plans in Cambodia. Lease agreements can range from a few months to several years.

Cost: Renting is typically a more affordable option, especially in the short term. Rental prices can vary greatly depending on the location and type of property.

Less Responsibility: As a tenant, you aren't responsible for property taxes or most maintenance and repair costs.

Buying in Cambodia:

Investment Opportunity: Purchasing property can be a solid investment if the real estate market is strong. However, it's essential to do thorough research or seek advice from a real estate professional before buying.

Control Over Property: As a homeowner, you have control over your property and can customize it to your liking.
Strata Titles: In 2010, the Cambodian government passed a law allowing foreigners to own properties above the ground floor (known as "strata titles") in buildings with a co-owned structure. However, land ownership is generally restricted to Cambodian citizens.

Potential Challenges: Buying property in Cambodia can come with challenges. The real estate market may be less regulated than in Western countries, and property rights can be complicated. It's crucial to work with a reputable real estate agent and legal professional to navigate this process. Remember, the decision between renting and buying should be based on your personal circumstances, including your financial situation, long-term plans, and comfort level with the local real estate market.

Please remember that the housing market and regulations can change. Always consult the latest resources or a real estate professional for the most accurate information.

6.2 Typical Housing Costs

When planning your move to Cambodia, understanding the typical housing costs is essential. Please note that these are approximate costs and actual prices can vary.

Renting Costs:

In popular areas for expats such as Phnom Penh and Siem Reap, you might expect to pay the following:

- A one-bedroom apartment in the city center: $250 - $500 per month
- A one-bedroom apartment outside the city center: $150 - $300 per month
- A three-bedroom apartment in the city center: $800 - $1,500 per month
- A three-bedroom apartment outside the city center: $400 - $800 per month

Keep in mind that these prices can fluctuate based on factors like the specific location, the property's condition, and whether utilities are included in the rent.

Buying Costs:
Purchasing property in Cambodia can vary greatly in cost, depending on the location, type, and size of the property. As a rough guide:

A condo in a modern development in central Phnom Penh: $1,500 - $2,500 per square meter

A villa or townhouse in central Phnom Penh: $2,000 - $3,000 per square meter

Please note, due to foreign ownership restrictions, most expats who buy property in Cambodia opt for condominiums in co-owned buildings, as mentioned in section 6.1.

Additional Costs:

Whether you're renting or buying, don't forget to factor in additional costs such as utility bills, property management fees (if buying in a co-owned building), maintenance costs, and, for buyers, property taxes and transaction fees.

Remember, property costs can change, and this information might be outdated. Always consult the latest resources or a real estate professional for the most accurate information.

6.3 Choosing a Location

Choosing the right location for your home in Cambodia can greatly influence your experience as an expat. Here are a few aspects to consider:

Urban vs. Rural: Would you prefer to live in a bustling city or peaceful countryside? Major cities like Phnom Penh, Siem Reap, and Sihanoukville offer a wide range of services, including international schools, restaurants, nightlife, and healthcare facilities. Rural areas offer a quieter, slower pace of life but may lack some amenities and can be far from healthcare facilities.

Proximity to Work or School: Depending on where you or your children are working or studying, it might be beneficial to live nearby to avoid long commutes.

Expatriate Communities: Areas with significant expat communities can offer a sense of familiarity and camaraderie, as well as amenities that cater to foreigners. In Phnom Penh, the neighborhoods of BKK1 and Tonle Bassac are popular with expats.

Safety: While Cambodia is generally safe, like any country, some areas are safer than others. Check with locals, other expats, or your country's embassy or consulate for up-to-date safety information about different neighborhoods.

Lifestyle Preferences: If you enjoy beach living, consider coastal areas like Sihanoukville or Kep. For those who prefer cultural and historical attractions, Siem Reap, home to Angkor Wat, might be the perfect choice.

Remember, where you choose to live should reflect your lifestyle, needs, and preferences. Spend some time visiting different areas before settling on the one that feels like the best fit for you.

Please remember that the safety and popularity of different areas can change. Always consult the latest resources or a real estate professional for the most accurate information.

6.4 Utilities and Other Expenses

In addition to your rent or mortgage, there are other essential living costs that you'll need to budget for when living in Cambodia. Here are some of the key expenses:

Utilities: Basic utilities, including electricity, water, garbage collection, and cooling (considering Cambodia's hot climate, a functioning air conditioner is almost a necessity), can cost around $50 to $150 per month for an average-sized apartment. These costs can fluctuate based on usage and the size of your home.

Internet: High-speed internet is widely available in Cambodia, particularly in urban areas. The cost for internet service is approximately $10 to $30 per month, depending on the speed and data package you choose.

Cable/Satellite TV: While not a necessity, if you wish to have a wider range of international TV channels, you can subscribe to cable or satellite TV. The costs can vary but expect to pay around $10 to $25 per month.

Housekeeping: Many expats in Cambodia choose to employ housekeepers or domestic helpers. Salaries can vary depending on whether the help is live-in or part-time, their responsibilities, and other factors, but expect to pay approximately $120 to $200 per month.

Maintenance: If you're renting, your landlord will typically take care of major repairs. However, you might be responsible for minor maintenance tasks. If you're a homeowner, all maintenance responsibilities will fall on you, so be sure to budget for this.

Please note that these are average costs and actual costs can vary. Always consult the latest resources or speak with locals for the most accurate information.

6.5 Land and Property Laws for Expats

When it comes to owning property in Cambodia, there are specific laws and regulations that expatriates should be aware of:

Foreign Ownership Restrictions: According to Cambodian law, foreigners cannot own land outright. However, they can legally own properties above the ground floor (excluding the land) in co-owned buildings, known as "strata titles." This typically applies to condominium units in multi-story buildings.

Lease Agreements: Another popular option for foreigners is to enter into long-term lease agreements, which can be for up to 50 years and are renewable. This method is often used by foreigners who wish to own standalone houses or villas.

Setting Up a Company: Foreigners can also opt to set up a legal entity, such as a limited company, to purchase property. In this scenario, the property is technically owned by the company. However, foreigners must partner with one or more Cambodian citizens who collectively own 51% of the shares.

Due Diligence: Whether you're buying or leasing property, it's important to conduct thorough due diligence. Check the title deeds, ensure there are no outstanding mortgages or disputes on the property, and confirm that the person selling or leasing the property is the legal owner.

Legal Advice: It's strongly recommended that you seek advice from a reputable legal professional when dealing with property transactions in Cambodia to ensure that you fully understand your rights and responsibilities and that the transaction is conducted legally and smoothly.

Please note that the laws and regulations regarding land and property ownership can change. Always consult the latest resources or a legal professional for the most accurate information.

6.6 Finding and Evaluating Property

Finding the right property in Cambodia involves several steps:

Online Research: Start your property search online. Websites like Khmer24, Realestate.com.kh, and IPS Cambodia list properties for sale and rent across the country. Use these platforms to get an idea of what is available in your price range and preferred locations.

Real Estate Agents: Consider hiring a reputable real estate agent, who can guide you through the process, negotiate on your behalf, and ensure that all paperwork is in order. An agent with experience serving expat clients can be particularly helpful.

Visiting Properties: Don't rely on photos alone. Make sure to visit properties in person to check their condition and get a feel for the neighborhood. This is also a good time to ask about any additional costs, such as service charges for condos.

Negotiating the Price: Whether you're renting or buying, don't be afraid to negotiate the price. It's common practice in Cambodia and could potentially save you a lot of money.

Conducting an Inspection: If you're buying a property, consider hiring a professional to conduct a thorough property inspection. They can identify any potential issues that might not be apparent during a casual walkthrough.

Legal Assistance: As mentioned in section 6.5, it's highly recommended to seek legal advice to ensure that all paperwork is in order and that the transaction is conducted legally.

Please note that the process of finding and evaluating properties can change. Always consult the latest resources or real estate professionals for the most accurate information.

7. Cost of Living

7.1 Typical Monthly Expenses

Understanding the typical monthly expenses can help you plan your budget effectively as an expat in Cambodia. Here is a general breakdown of what you might expect:

Housing: Rent for a one-bedroom apartment in city centers can range from $250 to $600 per month, while outside the city center, you could find rents as low as $150 to $400 per month. The cost of buying property varies widely depending on location, size, and type.

Utilities: As mentioned in section 6.4, utilities including electricity, water, cooling, and garbage collection, can cost around $50 to $150 per month.

Food: Dining out in local restaurants is quite affordable in Cambodia, with meals costing as little as $2 to $5 per dish. Western-style restaurants will be more expensive, with meals costing around $10 to $15. Grocery costs will vary depending on dietary habits, but generally, expect to spend around $200 to $400 per month.

Transportation: The cost of transportation can vary widely depending on the mode of transport. Tuk-tuk rides within the city can cost around $1 to $5 per trip. If you use a private car, you'll need to budget for fuel, maintenance, and insurance. Internet and Mobile Phone: High-speed internet can cost between $10 to $30 per month. A local mobile phone package with a generous data allowance could cost around $5 to $15 per month.

Entertainment and Leisure: Costs for entertainment and leisure activities will depend on personal preferences. Cinema tickets are around $4, while a gym membership can cost around $20 to $60 per month.

Healthcare: Costs for healthcare will depend on the type and level of insurance coverage you have. Out-of-pocket expenses can range from $15 to $30 for a doctor's visit to several hundred dollars for more complex treatments.

Please note that these are average costs and actual costs can vary. Always consult the latest resources or speak with locals for the most accurate information.

7.2 Cost of Food and Groceries

Food is an essential part of the monthly budget. In Cambodia, you can enjoy a rich variety of cuisines at different price points, and groceries are generally affordable, especially if you shop at local markets.

Eating Out: A meal at an inexpensive local restaurant can cost between $2 to $5, while a three-course meal for two at a mid-range restaurant might cost around $20 to $30. Western food tends to be more expensive, with prices like those in Western countries.

Groceries: Shopping for groceries at local markets can be quite economical. Here are some average prices for common items:

- A kilogram of rice: $0.50 to $1
- A dozen eggs: $1.50 to $2
- A kilogram of chicken breast: $3 to $4
- A kilogram of apples: $2 to $3
- A kilogram of tomatoes: $1 to $2
- A liter of milk: $1.50 to $2

Street Food: Cambodia is famous for its street food, which is not only delicious but also very affordable. You can find a wide variety of snacks, meals, and desserts for $1 to $3.

Drinks: The price of a domestic beer in restaurants is usually around $0.50 to $1.5, while imported beer can be $1 to $2.5. A regular cappuccino might cost you around $1.5 to $2.5.

Please remember that these prices are estimates and can vary depending on the location and the establishment. Prices in tourist-heavy areas are often higher than in other areas.

Always consult the latest resources or speak with locals for the most accurate information.

7.3 Cost of Transportation

Transportation costs in Cambodia can vary greatly depending on your chosen mode of transport, the distance traveled, and whether you are in a city or rural area.

Tuk-tuks and Moto-taxis: These are very popular modes of transportation, especially for short distances in cities. A tuk-tuk ride can cost between $1 and $5, while a moto-taxi (motorbike taxi) ride can be slightly cheaper. Bargaining is commonplace for these modes of transportation.

Taxis: Metered taxis are more common in Phnom Penh and can cost around $0.50 per kilometer, with a minimum fare of around $1.50 to $2.

Private Car: If you own a car, gasoline prices are around $0.95 per liter (or about $3.60 per gallon). However, owning a car in Cambodia can be expensive, considering the cost of the car itself, insurance, and maintenance.

Bicycles and Motorbikes: These are an affordable alternative for getting around. You can rent a bicycle for as little as $1 to $3 per day, and motorbikes for $5 to $10 per day.

Public Buses: In cities like Phnom Penh and Siem Reap, public buses are an extremely cost-effective way to get around, with fares typically costing $0.25 per trip. However, these services can be limited in other areas.

Long-distance Travel: For travel between cities, buses and minivans are commonly used. Prices vary based on the distance and comfort level but expect to pay between $5 to $15 for a bus ticket from Phnom Penh to Siem Reap, for example.

Keep in mind these prices are subject to change and can vary. Always consult the latest resources or speak with locals for the most accurate information.

7.4 Leisure and Entertainment Costs

Costs for leisure and entertainment in Cambodia can vary significantly based on your interests and lifestyle. Here are some general estimates:

Cinema Tickets: Going to the cinema can be a fun pastime. A ticket for a new release can cost around $3 to $5. Some cinemas also offer 4D experiences, which can cost around $8 to $12.

Gym Membership: Health and fitness centers are increasingly popular in larger cities such as Phnom Penh and Siem Reap. The cost of a monthly membership can range from around $20 to $60, depending on the facilities offered.

Nightlife: Nightlife in the larger cities is vibrant and varied. A beer at a local pub or bar can cost $1 to $2.5, while cocktails can range from $3 to $5. Entry fees for clubs can vary, with some places offering free entrance and others charging up to $10, often with a drink included.

Outdoor Activities: Cambodia is renowned for its natural beauty and historic sites. Entrance fees for natural parks or attractions can range from $1 to $10. A visit to the Angkor Wat archaeological park, for example, costs $37 for a one-day pass.

Cultural Activities: Museums and galleries typically charge an entrance fee, which can range from $1 to $5. Traditional Apsara dance shows, which often include a meal, can cost around $12 to $25.

Classes and Workshops: Cooking classes, language lessons, craft workshops, etc., can cost anywhere from $10 to $50, depending on the duration and the materials provided.

Please remember that these costs are estimates. Always consult the latest resources or speak with locals for the most accurate information.

7.5 Tax Considerations

Understanding the tax system in Cambodia is crucial for expats to plan their finances and to comply with local laws. Here are some key points to consider:

Income Tax: Residents in Cambodia are taxed on their worldwide income. Non-residents are taxed only on their Cambodian-sourced income. The tax rates are progressive, ranging from 0% to 20% based on your income bracket.

Value-Added Tax (VAT): Cambodia has a flat VAT rate of 10% that applies to goods and services.

Property Tax: Owners of immovable property in Cambodia are subject to an annual property tax. The tax is levied at 0.1% on the market value of the property exceeding KHR 100 million (around $25,000), excluding the value of the land.

Withholding Tax: Various types of payments to residents and non-residents are subject to withholding tax. These include rental income, interest, royalties, and services fees.

Import Duties and Taxes: Cambodia has import duties on certain goods brought into the country. The rates can vary depending on the nature and value of the goods.

Please note that tax laws can be complex and are subject to change. This is only a general guide, and you should consult with a tax professional or an international tax consultancy to understand how the Cambodian tax laws will apply to your specific situation. Always comply with local laws and regulations and keep up to date with the latest information.

8. Education

8.1 Overview of the Education System

The education system in Cambodia has seen significant improvements in the past few decades, although it still faces challenges.

Structure: Cambodia's education system is divided into general education, technical education, and higher education. General education includes pre-school, primary education (grades 1 to 6), lower secondary education (grades 7 to 9), and upper secondary education (grades 10 to 12).

Curriculum: The core curriculum at the primary and secondary levels includes Khmer language, mathematics, social sciences, natural sciences, physical education, and arts. English is often introduced as a second language from the primary level onwards.

Access: Enrollment rates in primary education are high, but dropout rates increase in secondary education, especially in rural areas. The government, with the aid of international organizations, has been implementing programs to increase enrollment and retention rates in secondary schools.

Quality and Challenges: Although progress has been made, the quality of education in Cambodia is still a challenge. This is due to factors such as inadequate infrastructure, shortage of trained teachers, large class sizes, and limited resources.

International Schools: For expatriate families, there are several international schools, particularly in Phnom Penh and Siem Reap, that offer education in English or other languages and follow internationally recognized curricula such as the International Baccalaureate (IB) or the American, British, and French curricula.

It's important for expats to research the best options for their children, considering factors such as curriculum, tuition fees, location, facilities, and the school's accreditation status.

8.2 International and Local Schools

In Cambodia, expats have the option to choose between local schools and international schools, each offering a distinct learning environment and opportunities.

Local Schools: These institutions follow the national curriculum set by Cambodia's Ministry of Education, Youth and Sport. The language of instruction in local schools is Khmer. While tuition fees in public schools are generally low, these schools often face challenges like overcrowded classrooms, limited resources, and a shortage of well-trained teachers. It's also important to note that the local educational approach can be quite different from Western standards, focusing more on rote learning rather than critical thinking and problem-solving skills.

International Schools: These are often the go-to choose for expat families due to the language barrier in local schools. International schools in Cambodia offer a range of curricula, including the International Baccalaureate (IB), British, American, Australian, French, and Japanese among others. They also provide a more familiar educational setting for expat children, focusing on a broad range of skills and global citizenship. Some popular international schools include the Northbridge International School, International School Phnom Penh (ISPP), and British International School of Phnom Penh. However, international schools come with significantly higher tuition fees. It's not uncommon for fees to range from $5,000 to $20,000 per year, depending on the age of the student and the school chosen. Some families might find it worthwhile for the quality of education, range of extracurricular activities, and the multicultural environment that can ease the adaptation process for their children.

In choosing between local and international schools, consider factors such as your child's language proficiency, your financial capability, the length of your stay in Cambodia, and your child's adaptability to new environments.

8.3 Schooling Options for Expat Children

Choosing the right schooling option for your children is one of the most important decisions you'll make as an expat. In Cambodia, there are several options available depending on your family's needs, your child's educational background:

International Schools: As mentioned, international schools offer a curriculum like what your child might experience back home or in other international settings, often following recognized programs like the International Baccalaureate, British, American, or French curricula. They also offer a diverse environment with students from many different nationalities.

Local Schools: While the language of instruction (Khmer) and teaching methods can be a barrier, enrolling your child in a local school offers a deep and authentic immersion into Cambodian society and culture. It could be an option to consider if your child is proficient in Khmer or if you plan to stay in the country for the long term.

Bilingual Schools: These schools offer instruction in both Khmer and English (or other languages), providing a middle ground between local and international schools. They can be a good choice if you want your child to maintain their home language while also learning Khmer.

Home-schooling: Some expat families choose to home-school their children, either following a curriculum from their home country or using international online programs. This gives families more control over their children's education but requires a significant time commitment and might limit social interactions with peers.

Online/Distant Learning: As technology continues to improve, so does the viability of online learning. This could be a good option if traditional schooling options don't fit your family's needs or if you're moving frequently.

Remember that each child is unique, and what works for one might not work for another. It's crucial to involve your child in the decision process as much as possible and consider their feelings, adaptability, and educational needs when choosing a schooling option.

8.4 Adult and Continuing Education Opportunities

As an expat in Cambodia, you might be interested in furthering your education or learning new skills. The good news is there are a variety of opportunities for adult and continuing education in the country:

Universities: Cambodia's universities, such as the Royal University of Phnom Penh or Pannasastra University, offer undergraduate, postgraduate, and doctoral programs in a variety of fields. While instruction is often in Khmer, some institutions offer courses in English.

Language Courses: Language skills are invaluable for expats. Institutions like the Institute of Foreign Languages (IFL) offer language courses, including Khmer and English. Private tutors are also an option if you prefer one-on-one instruction.

Professional Development: There are several organizations and companies that offer short courses, workshops, and training programs to develop your professional skills. Fields can range from project management and IT to marketing and entrepreneurship.

Cooking and Art Classes: If you're looking to learn about Cambodian culture, consider taking cooking or traditional art classes. These can be a fun way to spend your time and learn about the local culture.

Online Courses: With the rise of online learning platforms like Coursera, Khan Academy, or Udemy, you can study virtually anything from anywhere.

When considering further education, consider factors such as your personal goals, the credibility of the institution, the cost, and the language of instruction. It's also a good idea to check if your qualifications will be recognized both in Cambodia and your home country.

8.5 Cultural Immersion and Learning Khmer

As an expat in Cambodia, immersing yourself in the local culture and learning the local language can significantly enrich your experience. Here are some suggestions:

Learning Khmer: While English is commonly spoken in tourist areas and international settings, knowing some Khmer will help you in day-to-day life, make local friends, and show respect to the local culture. You can take classes, hire a private tutor, or use language learning apps. For a more immersive experience, language exchange meetups, where locals and expats teach each other their languages, are becoming more popular in cities like Phnom Penh and Siem Reap.

Cultural Classes and Workshops: Participating in cultural classes or workshops can provide a deeper understanding of Cambodian culture. This could include traditional dance, music, or arts and crafts classes.

Festivals and Public Celebrations: Engaging in local celebrations like the Khmer New Year or the Water Festival is a wonderful way to experience Cambodian culture firsthand.

Volunteering: Contributing to community projects or local non-profits can offer a unique perspective on Cambodian society while allowing you to give back to your host community.

Local Tours: Taking tours guided by locals can give you insight into aspects of the culture that you might not discover otherwise.

Remember, cultural immersion is a process, and even small steps toward understanding can make your experience as an expat more rewarding.

9. Work and Business

9.1 Employment Opportunities and Job Market Overview

Finding gainful employment is a crucial part of the expat experience, and in Cambodia, the job market presents a mixed bag of opportunities and challenges.

Industries with High Demand: The highest demand for foreign workers in Cambodia tends to be in the fields of education (especially English language teaching), tourism, NGOs, and international business. The growing technology and startup sector is also increasingly open to foreign expertise. Skills in these areas could potentially lead to job opportunities.

English Teaching: There is a high demand for English teachers across the country. Positions are available in international schools, private language institutions, and even within some local schools. Qualifications required may vary, with some institutions requiring TEFL certification or equivalent, and others seeking experienced teachers with education-related degrees.

NGOs and International Organizations: Cambodia is home to a multitude of NGOs and international organizations that often hire foreign employees. These organizations cover a broad range of sectors including health, education, human rights, and development.

Tourism and Hospitality: With its rich history and culture, Cambodia is a major destination for international tourists. Jobs in this sector can range from hotel management to tour guiding, especially for individuals who can bring language skills and international experience to the table.

Business and Finance: As Cambodia's economy continues to grow, there are increasing opportunities for foreign professionals in business, finance, and related sectors. Particularly, Phnom Penh has a growing need for professionals with experience in international business practices.

While the demand for foreign workers is present, it's important to keep in mind that the job market in Cambodia is competitive. Also, salaries, while increasing, may still be lower compared to Western standards. Before you embark on your job search, it's wise to research thoroughly, establish contacts where possible, and be open to various opportunities.

9.2 Professional Qualifications and Certifications

As an expat seeking employment in Cambodia, your professional qualifications and certifications can play a significant role in your job search:

Degree Recognition: Cambodian employers generally recognize degrees from international universities. However, it's always wise to check in advance if there are any specific validation requirements for your field, especially for regulated professions like medicine or law.

TEFL Certification: For those interested in teaching English, a TEFL (Teaching English as a Foreign Language) certification can be an asset. Some institutions may require it, while others may just prefer it. Some TEFL courses can be taken online, but in-person courses are generally seen as more credible. Proficiency in English: Being fluent in English is often an asset in Cambodia's job market. It's the language of business in many sectors and is particularly useful in tourism, education, and international organizations.

Language Proficiency: Beyond English, knowledge of other languages such as French, Chinese, Japanese or Korean can open job opportunities, particularly in the tourism and hospitality sectors. Proficiency in Khmer can also be a huge plus, showing commitment to integrating into the local culture.

Professional Licenses: For some professions, you'll need to transfer or validate your professional licenses. This is common in healthcare professions, law, and teaching. The requirements can vary, so it's crucial to check with relevant local or professional bodies.

Local Certifications: For certain roles, you might need to acquire local certifications. For example, if you want to guide tours, you'll need to get a license from the Ministry of Tourism. It's also important to note that networking can be invaluable when job hunting in Cambodia. Many jobs are filled through word of mouth, so making connections in your field can greatly aid your job search.

9.3 Starting a Business in Cambodia

Starting a business in a new country can be an exciting endeavor, and Cambodia, with its developing economy, offers several opportunities. Here are some things to consider:

Business Opportunities: Sectors like tourism, agriculture, real estate, and tech startups are seeing a rise in investment. Identifying a unique business idea that caters to a need in these sectors could prove successful.

Legal Structure: Businesses in Cambodia can be set up as sole proprietorships, private limited companies, public limited companies, partnerships, or representative offices. The choice of legal structure will depend on factors like the nature of your business, the level of liability you are willing to assume, and tax implications.

Registration Process: The process of registering a business involves several steps. You will need to register with the Ministry of Commerce, the Tax Department of the Ministry of Economy and Finance, and possibly other governmental departments depending on your business type. The process can be complex, so you might consider hiring a local legal firm to guide you through it.

Capital Requirements: For some types of companies, the law requires a minimum amount of registered capital. Be sure to understand these requirements before proceeding.

Licenses and Permits: Depending on the nature of your business, you may need to obtain specific licenses or permits. This could range from health and safety permits for restaurants to tour operator licenses for travel companies.

Local Partnerships: It's often beneficial to seek local business partners who understand the market and can navigate the local business landscape. They can provide insights into customer behaviors, business customs, and help avoid potential pitfalls.

Challenges: While there are many opportunities, starting a business in Cambodia can also present challenges. These might include navigating local bureaucracy, understanding local business customs, and dealing with infrastructure issues. Before deciding to start a business, do thorough market research, understand the legal and regulatory environment, and consider seeking advice from business consultants or legal professionals.

9.4 Labor Laws and Employee Rights

Cambodia's labor laws are designed to protect the rights of workers and dictate the obligations of employers. As an expat, you should be aware of the following key aspects of labor law:

Working Hours: The standard working hours in Cambodia are 8 hours per day or 48 hours per week. For overtime work, employees are entitled to additional pay.

Public Holidays and Leave: Employees are entitled to annual leave of 1.5 days per month of work. There are also several public holidays throughout the year, during which employees are entitled to a day off with full pay.

Minimum Wage: There's a minimum wage in Cambodia, but it currently only applies to the garment and footwear sector. In other sectors, wages are generally a matter of agreement between the employer and the employee.

Termination and Severance Pay: The Labor Law provides regulations on termination of employment contracts and entitles employees to severance pay under certain conditions.

Social Security: Cambodia has a social security scheme that provides benefits for occupational accidents, healthcare, and pensions. Both employers and employees contribute to this scheme.

Trade Unions: Employees in Cambodia have the right to form and join trade unions. Trade unions play a significant role in the garment and footwear industry but are less prevalent in other sectors.

Work Permits: As mentioned earlier, all foreigners are required to have a work permit and employment card to work legally in Cambodia. Employers are usually responsible for arranging these.

While these points provide a general overview, it's advisable to get more detailed information based on your specific circumstances, potentially consulting with a legal professional. Please note that these labor laws may not cover self-employed individuals or business owners.

9.5 Income Tax Considerations

Income earned while working in Cambodia, whether by residents or non-residents, is subject to income tax. Here are some key points to understand:

Residency Status: An individual is considered a resident for tax purposes if they reside in Cambodia for more than 182 days in a calendar year. Residents are taxed on their worldwide income, while non-residents are taxed only on their Cambodian-sourced income.

Income Tax Rates: For residents, the tax rate is progressive, ranging from 0% to 20% based on income brackets. Non-residents are subject to a flat rate of 20% on their Cambodian-sourced income.

Tax Deductions: Certain deductions are available when calculating taxable income, including personal deductions for the taxpayer, spouse, and dependents. There are also deductions for social security contributions and premiums for life insurance policies issued in Cambodia.

Tax Filing: Income tax returns should be filed, and taxes paid no later than three months after the end of the tax year. The tax year in Cambodia is the calendar year.

Double Taxation Agreements: Cambodia has double taxation agreements with a few countries to avoid double taxation for individuals and companies. Check if your home country has such an agreement with Cambodia.

Self-Employed and Business Taxes: If you're self-employed or own a business, you may also be subject to additional taxes, such as value-added tax (VAT), withholding tax, and prepayment of income tax.

It's important to note that tax laws can be complex and subject to change. Therefore, it's always advisable to consult with a tax professional or an accountant to understand your tax obligations fully.

9.6 Networking and Professional Groups

In any new country, establishing a strong professional network can open doors to new opportunities, and Cambodia is no different. Here are a few ways to build and strengthen your network:

Business Associations: Several international business associations operate in Cambodia, such as the British Business Association of Cambodia (BBAC), EuroCham, and the Australian Business Association of Cambodia (ABAC). Joining these groups can provide opportunities for networking and can offer valuable insights into doing business in the country.

Networking Events: Many organizations and venues in major cities like Phnom Penh and Siem Reap host networking events. These events often cater to specific industries, so find those relevant to your field.

Local Meetups: Attending local meetups, whether based around professional, cultural, or recreational interests, can be a great way to meet people from a variety of backgrounds.

Websites like Meetup.com and Facebook groups can be good sources of information.

LinkedIn: Don't underestimate the power of online networking. LinkedIn can be a valuable tool for making professional connections in Cambodia.

Volunteering: Volunteering can be a meaningful way to meet people and give back to the community. Many NGOs in Cambodia welcome the expertise of professionals in a range of fields.

Remember, networking isn't just about taking—it's about building genuine relationships and finding ways to offer help and value to others. By approaching networking with an open mind and a willingness to contribute, you'll likely find it a rewarding aspect of your professional life in Cambodia.

10. Language and Culture

10.1 Cultural Norms and Etiquette

Understanding the local culture and norms is key to integrating into any society, and Cambodia is no exception. Here are some important aspects of Cambodian culture and etiquette: Respect and Politeness: Cambodians place a high value on respect and politeness. Traditional greetings involve placing the hands together in a prayer-like gesture called a 'sampeah', with the height of the hands and the depth of the bow varying based on the status of the person you're greeting.

Hierarchy: Cambodian society is quite hierarchical. Age, job position, and social status often determine how people interact with each other.

Dress Code: Modesty in clothing is appreciated, especially when visiting religious sites like temples, where shoulders and knees should be covered. Business attire is typically formal.

Personal Space: Cambodians generally respect personal space. Touching someone on the head, even as a friendly gesture, is considered disrespectful because the head is viewed as the most sacred part of the body.

Communication Style: Cambodians often employ indirect communication to avoid conflict and maintain harmony. They may avoid saying 'no' directly, preferring to give evasive or non-committal answers instead.

Table Manners: It's customary to wait for the host or elder to start eating before others begin. When eating with a spoon and fork, the spoon is held in the right hand and the fork in the left.

Gift-Giving: Gifts are typically given and received with both hands. It's also polite to refuse a gift once or twice before accepting it.

As with any culture, norms can vary, and learning comes through observation and interaction with locals. Cambodians are generally forgiving of minor etiquette mistakes, if they see that you are respectful and trying to understand their culture.

10.2 Holidays and Festivals

Cambodia has a rich tradition of festivals and holidays that reflect the country's cultural, religious, and historical heritage. Here are a few of the key events:

Khmer New Year (Choul Chnam Thmey): Celebrated in mid-April, this is one of Cambodia's most important holidays, marking the end of the harvest season. It is a time for family gatherings, temple visits, and traditional games.

Pchum Ben: Held in September or October, Pchum Ben is a 15-day religious festival where Cambodians pay respect to their ancestors. Many people visit temples and make offerings of food and gifts to the spirits of their deceased relatives.

Water Festival (Bon Om Touk): This November festival celebrates the reversal of the flow of the Tonle Sap River. It includes boat races, concerts, and fireworks. The festival often attracts large crowds to Phnom Penh.

Royal Ploughing Ceremony (Pithi Chrat Preah Neanng Korl): An ancient royal rite held in May to mark the start of the rice-growing season. The ceremony is meant to predict the success of the upcoming harvest.

Visak Bochea: Celebrated in April or May, this Buddhist holiday commemorates the birth, enlightenment, and death of Buddha.

Independence Day: Held on November 9, this public holiday celebrates Cambodia's independence from France in 1953.

King's Birthday: The King's Birthday is a national holiday that spans three days in May. The celebrations include fireworks, parades, and a large gathering outside the Royal Palace. These holidays provide valuable insights into the cultural and religious life of Cambodians. Participating in or observing these celebrations can be a great way to understand and respect the traditions and customs of your new home.

10.3 Religion and Its Role in Cambodian Culture

Religion plays a central role in Cambodian life, shaping its customs, traditions, and social norms. Here's what you need to know:

Buddhism: Most Cambodians, about 97%, follow Theravada Buddhism, which influences many aspects of daily life, from moral conduct to ceremonial rituals. Monks in saffron robes are a common sight, and you will find numerous pagodas, or 'wats', across the country. Many Cambodians visit these religious sites regularly to pray and make offerings.

Religious Holidays and Festivals: Many Cambodian holidays are rooted in Buddhist traditions. The Buddhist calendar, which is lunisolar, dictates the dates of many festivals, such as Khmer New Year, Pchum Ben, and Visak Bochea. These celebrations often involve family gatherings, temple visits, and acts of merit-making, like giving to the poor and offering food to monks.

Monastic Life: Many Cambodian men, regardless of their background, spend part of their lives as Buddhist monks. This practice is seen as a rite of passage and an act of merit for their families.

Ancestor Worship: Alongside Buddhism, belief in ancestral spirits is also prevalent. Many homes have spirit houses or shrines where daily offerings are made to appease the spirits and seek their blessings.

Other Religions: While Buddhism is dominant, there are also small populations of Muslims, Christians, and followers of indigenous animist beliefs.

Respect for Religion: It's essential to show respect for religious customs and practices. For instance, dress modestly when visiting temples, remove your shoes before entering religious buildings, and avoid touching or disrespecting images of Buddha.

As an expat, understanding the role of religion in Cambodian society can help you better appreciate the culture, traditions, and mindset of its people.

10.4 Integrating into the Local Community

Building a strong connection with the local community can make your time in Cambodia more fulfilling and enriching. Here are some tips to help you integrate:

Learn Khmer: While English is increasingly spoken, particularly in urban areas and tourist spots, learning the local language, Khmer, can open doors to deeper connections and understanding. Even learning basic phrases can be a sign of respect and an effort to assimilate.

Join Local Events and Festivals: As mentioned earlier, Cambodia has a vibrant cultural scene with numerous holidays and festivals. Participation in these public events can be a great way to understand local customs and traditions.

Get Involved with Community Projects: Volunteering for local community projects or NGOs can offer opportunities to interact closely with locals and contribute positively to your new home.

Respect Local Customs and Traditions: Showing respect for local customs, traditions, and religious practices is critical. This includes dressing modestly, especially when visiting temples, understanding local etiquette, and being mindful of the country's history and sensitivities.

Try Local Cuisine: Food is a significant part of any culture, and Cambodian cuisine is no exception. Going beyond popular dishes like amok and trying a variety of local foods can be a delightful cultural experience.

Support Local Businesses: Shopping at local markets, eating at local eateries, and using local services can not only help the local economy but also provide more opportunities for cultural exchange.

Patience and Open-mindedness: Adapting to a new culture can be challenging. There might be practices and norms that are quite different from what you're used to. Approaching these differences with patience and an open mind can go a long way in helping you adapt.

Remember, integrating into the local community doesn't mean losing your cultural identity. It's about finding a balance between maintaining your own traditions and adopting new ones, creating a rich and unique expat experience.

10.5 Cultural Norms and Etiquette

Cambodian society is steeped in tradition, respect, and courtesy. Understanding local cultural norms and etiquette is essential to building good relationships and integrating into Cambodian society. Here are some key points to remember: Respect for Elders: Cambodian culture is heavily influenced by hierarchical societal structures. Elders are highly respected, and deference to those older or in higher social positions is expected.

The Sampeah: This traditional Khmer greeting involves placing your palms together in a prayer-like gesture and bowing slightly. The position of your hands and the depth of your bow depends on the social status or age of the person you're greeting.

Modesty: Modest dress is appreciated, particularly in rural areas. This is especially important when visiting religious sites, where shoulders and knees should be covered.
Politeness: Politeness is highly valued. Raised voices and displays of anger are seen as a loss of face and are generally avoided. It is better to approach situations calmly and with a smile.

Head and Feet: The head is considered the highest and most sacred part of the body, while the feet are considered the lowest. As such, touching someone's head or pointing with your feet can be seen as disrespectful.

Giving and Receiving: When giving or receiving something, use both hands and your right hand, never your left hand alone. This applies to passing objects, money, or business cards.

Temple Etiquette: When visiting temples, dress modestly, remove your shoes before entering, and avoid touching or disrespecting images of Buddha. If monks are present, give them space and do not touch them, especially if you're a woman, as monks are not allowed to touch women.

These norms provide a framework, but remember that everyone's experience may differ, and cultural understanding grows with time and experience. It's always a good idea to observe and follow the lead of locals in social situations.

11. Practical Information

11.1 Transportation System

Cambodia offers a variety of transportation options, ranging from public to private transport. Here's an overview of the different modes available:

City Buses: In the capital, Phnom Penh, city buses have become a popular means of transportation. They are inexpensive and cover a broad network of routes across the city.

Taxis and Tuk Tuks: Taxis are readily available in major cities. For shorter distances, tuk tuks (three-wheeled taxis) are a common sight and an essential part of the Cambodian transportation scene. Always agree on the fare before starting your journey.

Ride-Hailing Apps: Apps like Grab and PassApp have gained popularity in cities, providing an easy way to hire taxis, tuk tuks, or even motorbikes.

Motorbikes: Motorbike rentals are popular among locals and expats for their convenience. However, traffic in Cambodia can be chaotic, so this option requires good riding skills and extra caution. Also, remember that by law, helmets are mandatory.

Bicycles: In smaller towns or for short distances, bicycles can be a cheap and eco-friendly alternative. Many places offer bicycle rentals for a small fee.

Boats and Ferries: For travel along the Mekong and Tonle Sap rivers, or to reach some of the islands, boats and ferries are often used.

Trains: Cambodia's train service is limited but can provide a scenic alternative for travel between some major towns. Long-Distance Buses: For intercity travel, long-distance buses are widely used. They are affordable and connect all major towns.

Air Travel: Domestic flights can be a quick but more expensive option for travelling between cities. Cambodia has several operational airports, including in Phnom Penh, Siem Reap, and Sihanoukville.

When using any mode of transport, be aware of safety standards, and always keep your belongings secure. Also, make sure to familiarize yourself with local traffic rules and customs if you plan to drive.

11.2 Internet and Telecommunications

Staying connected is essential, especially when living abroad. Here's what you need to know about internet and telecommunications in Cambodia:

Internet: Over the last decade, Cambodia has seen significant improvements in its internet infrastructure. In major cities like Phnom Penh, Siem Reap, and Sihanoukville, high-speed internet is readily available and reliable. Many coffee shops, restaurants, and hotels offer free Wi-Fi. For home use, numerous service providers offer broadband packages at varying prices.

Mobile Internet: For those on the move, mobile data plans are a popular choice. With the expansion of 4G networks across the country, you can expect decent mobile internet speed in most urban areas and many rural regions.

Telecommunications: Mobile phones are widely used in Cambodia. The country has several mobile operators, such as Cellcard, Metfone, and Smart Axiata, offering a range of prepaid and postpaid services. SIM cards can be bought easily upon arrival at the airport or from many local shops. Be prepared to provide a copy of your passport for registration.

International Calls: If you need to make international calls, VoIP services like Skype, WhatsApp, and Viber are commonly used. Some mobile operators also offer international calling packages.

Postal Services: The Cambodian postal service provides domestic and international mail services. However, for critical documents or packages, many expats prefer to use international courier services like DHL or FedEx for more reliable and trackable delivery.

Always remember to compare different providers and plans for internet and mobile services to find the one that best suits your needs and budget.

11.3 Local Cuisine

Experiencing the local cuisine is one of the joys of living in a new country, and Cambodia is no exception. Khmer cuisine is a delightful fusion of flavors, with influences from India, China, and neighboring Southeast Asian nations. Here are some must-try dishes and local food customs:

Amok: This is one of the most famous dishes in Cambodia. It's a creamy, coconut milk-based curry, typically made with fish, although chicken or tofu versions are also available. It is commonly steamed and served in a banana leaf cup.

Lok Lak: A delectable, stir-fried beef dish, served with fresh vegetables and a tangy lime and black pepper dipping sauce. It is often accompanied by a fried egg and served over rice.

Nom Banh Chok: Known as Khmer noodles, this is a popular breakfast dish. It consists of rice noodles topped with a fish-based green curry gravy, fresh mint leaves, bean sprouts, banana flower, cucumber, and other greens.

Street Food: Street food stalls and markets are integral parts of the culinary scene in Cambodia. They offer an array of dishes, from grilled meats and sticky rice to tropical fruits and sweet treats. Always remember to ensure the food is freshly cooked and the stall maintains good hygiene practices.

Dining Etiquette: Khmer dining etiquette is a blend of Asian traditions. It's common to use a fork and spoon for eating; chopsticks are typically used for noodle dishes. Meals are often served family-style, with several shared dishes.

Beverages: When it comes to drinks, 'teuk tnaot' (palm juice) and 'teuk kroch chhma' (rice wine) are local favorites. Coffee, often served iced, is also popular, as is beer.

Vegetarian/Vegan Options: While traditional Cambodian cuisine includes a lot of seafood and meats, most restaurants in urban areas offer vegetarian or vegan options.

Embrace the local cuisine, but also remember to pay attention to food safety. Avoid uncooked vegetables and ensure that your food has been cooked thoroughly, especially when eating street food. Bon appétit, or as the locals say, 'Nham Bay Te'!

11.4 Safety and Security Tips

When living abroad, personal safety and security should always be a priority. Here are some tips to keep you safe while living in Cambodia:

General Safety: Like many other countries, Cambodia has areas that are safer than others. Phnom Penh, Siem Reap, and other tourist-heavy cities have their fair share of petty crime, such as pickpocketing, especially in crowded places. Always be aware of your surroundings, avoid displaying expensive belongings, and ensure your accommodation is secure.

Road Safety: Traffic in Cambodia can be chaotic. If you are driving, always wear a helmet on motorbikes and ensure seat belts are worn in cars. Be alert for erratic driving behaviors.

Food and Water Safety: Tap water in Cambodia is not safe to drink. Always opt for bottled water and make sure the seal is not broken. Also, be careful with street food. Make sure the food is freshly cooked and served hot, and the stall maintains good hygiene practices.

Healthcare: While Cambodia's healthcare system has improved over the years, it's still not up to Western standards. It is recommended to get comprehensive health insurance that covers medical evacuation.

Scams: Like many tourist destinations, Cambodia has its share of scams. Be wary of overly friendly strangers, double-check your bills, and agree on prices before accepting services.

Natural Disasters: Cambodia is prone to monsoons and flooding, particularly between May and November. Keep an eye on local news and weather forecasts, and follow any advice or instructions given by local authorities.

Emergency Numbers: Make sure to have local emergency numbers saved on your phone. The general emergency number in Cambodia is 117.

Local Laws and Customs: Respect local customs, traditions, and laws. Some actions that might seem innocuous to you could be illegal or disrespectful in Cambodia. When in doubt, ask, observe, or do some research.

Remember, your safety is paramount, so always prioritize it above all else. Most Cambodians are incredibly welcoming and friendly, but as with any destination, it's important to stay vigilant and aware.

11.5 Shopping and Food

Whether you're looking for daily necessities, unique souvenirs, or a bite to eat, Cambodia offers a range of shopping and dining experiences. Here are some insights:

Markets: The heart of shopping in Cambodia is its bustling markets. For instance, the Central Market (Phsar Thmei) and Russian Market (Phsar Toul Tom Poung) in Phnom Penh, or the Old Market (Phsar Chas) in Siem Reap, are full of clothes, fresh produce, local handicrafts, and much more. Always remember that haggling is part of the shopping experience in these markets!

Supermarkets and Convenience Stores: For daily groceries, supermarkets such as AEON and Lucky Supermarket offer a wide variety of local and imported goods. Additionally, convenience stores like Circle K and Thai Huot Market can be found throughout urban areas.

Malls: For a more modern shopping experience, Cambodia's cities have seen an increase in the number of shopping malls. AEON Mall and Sorya Center Point in Phnom Penh, for example, house a variety of local and international brands.

Specialty Shops: There are also numerous specialty shops across Cambodia selling everything from home decor, books, to high-quality silk and artisan crafts. Artisans Angkor in Siem Reap is a well-known spot for quality Khmer crafts.

Food: From Khmer restaurants, international eateries, to street food stalls, you'll find a wide array of options catering to all taste buds and budgets in Cambodia. Do not miss out on trying local dishes like Fish Amok, Lok Lak, and Nom Banh Chok.

Eating Etiquette: When dining, remember that it's common in Cambodia to share dishes. Always use your own spoon when serving yourself from shared plates.

Tipping: Tipping isn't mandatory in Cambodia, but it's appreciated. In restaurants, a tip of around 10% is common if service charge isn't included in the bill.

Remember, shopping locally not only gives you a chance to interact with the local community but also supports the local economy. So, enjoy exploring the shopping and dining scene in Cambodia!

11.6 Pet Ownership and Animal Laws

Bringing your pet to Cambodia or adopting one once you're there can make your experience feel more like home. However, it's important to understand the local laws and considerations regarding pet ownership:

Bringing Pets into Cambodia: Cambodia allows the import of pets, including dogs and cats, from overseas. The pet must be microchipped, vaccinated against rabies at least 30 days (but not more than a year) prior to entry, and a health certificate must be issued by a licensed vet from your home country. It is recommended to check with your airline for any specific pet travel requirements.

Quarantine: There are no mandatory quarantine requirements for pets entering Cambodia. However, regulations can change, so always confirm with the relevant authorities before your move.

Veterinary Care: While vet care in Cambodia is improving, it may not be up to the standard you're used to, especially outside major cities. Research beforehand to find a reputable vet clinic in your area.

Pet-Friendly Accommodations: Not all accommodations in Cambodia allow pets, so make sure to check the pet policy if you're renting.

Local Customs and Regulations: Cambodians generally have a different attitude towards pets compared to Western countries. Free-roaming dogs and cats are common. It's essential to respect these local customs, even if they differ from your own.

Exotic Pets: Importing or owning certain exotic pets is prohibited in Cambodia. Always check with local authorities and ensure you're not supporting illegal wildlife trade.

Stray Animals: There is a significant population of stray animals in Cambodia. Several non-profit organizations work towards their rescue and care. You can consider volunteering, donating, or adopting from these organizations.

Pet Care During Hot Weather: Cambodia's tropical climate can be tough on pets. Ensure they have constant access to shade and fresh water and try to walk them during cooler parts of the day.

Having a pet in Cambodia can be a rewarding experience, but it's essential to be informed and prepared.

12. Life as an Expat

12.1 Expat Communities

Moving to a new country can be a daunting experience, and finding a group of people who are sharing a similar journey can be immensely comforting. Luckily, Cambodia has a vibrant and diverse expat community, particularly in cities like Phnom Penh and Siem Reap:

Expat Groups and Organizations: There are several expat groups and organizations in Cambodia, both formal and informal. These groups offer a platform to socialize, share experiences, and aid in navigating your new life in Cambodia. Some popular expat groups include the Cambodia Parent Network and Phnom Penh Expat Women.

Online Forums and Social Media: Social media platforms and online forums like the Cambodia Expats Online Forum and Facebook groups like Expats & Locals in Phnom Penh provide a virtual space for interaction and information exchange.

Networking Events: There are also various networking events, often organized by local businesses or expat groups, where you can meet other expats and locals.

Volunteering: Volunteering can be another great way to meet like-minded people and give back to the local community. Organizations such as Volunteer in Cambodia or Cambodia NGO offer numerous volunteering opportunities.

Remember, while it's comforting to connect with fellow expats, it's also vital to integrate into the local community. Learning the language, understanding the culture, and building relationships with locals will make your experience in Cambodia more fulfilling.

12.2 Making Local Friends

Befriending locals is one of the most rewarding aspects of expat life and can significantly enrich your time in Cambodia. Here are some ways you can build these important relationships:

Language Classes: Enrolling in Khmer language classes is not only beneficial for communication but is also a fantastic opportunity to meet locals who are often engaged as teachers and tutors.

Community Engagement: Participating in local events, festivals, and community projects can put you in touch with locals who share similar interests.

Neighborhood Interaction: Simple day-to-day activities, such as shopping at local markets or visiting neighborhood cafés, provide excellent opportunities to interact with Cambodian locals.

Workplace Relationships: If you're working in Cambodia, your colleagues can be an invaluable resource for navigating local customs and forming friendships.

Sports and Fitness Groups: Joining a local sports team, fitness class, or outdoor adventure group is a fun way to connect with locals who share similar interests.

Language Exchange Partners: Find a language exchange partner who wants to learn your language while teaching you Khmer.

Building friendships with locals may require stepping out of your comfort zone, and cultural differences may present challenges at times. However, the rewards of these relationships—deeper understanding of the culture, more profound integration into the community, and unique insights into Cambodian life—far outweigh the initial challenges.

12.3 Dealing with Homesickness

Despite the excitement of living in a new country, it's normal for expats to experience homesickness. This can manifest as a longing for familiar environments, people, or routines. Here are some strategies to cope with homesickness in Cambodia:

Stay Connected: Thankfully, technology makes it easier than ever to stay in touch with loved ones back home. Regular video calls, messages, or even social media updates can help you feel more connected.

Create Familiarity: Bring or find items from home that bring you comfort. This could be photos, favorite books, or even certain foods. Familiarity can provide a comforting touchstone when everything else seems new and overwhelming.

Explore Local Culture: Diving into Cambodian culture can help turn the unfamiliar into the familiar. Learn about the history, customs, food, and language of Cambodia. The more you understand, the more connected you'll feel.

Find Your Community: Connect with other expats who may be having the same experiences. Sharing your feelings with others who understand can provide a great deal of comfort.

Take Care of Your Health: Homesickness can take a toll on your physical health. Make sure to eat healthily, exercise regularly, and get enough sleep. If you're feeling persistently low, don't hesitate to seek professional help.

Plan Visits Home: If possible, plan visits back home. Having a trip to look forward to can make a big difference.
Remember, it's okay to feel homesick—it's a normal part of the adjustment process. With time, the unfamiliar will become familiar, and Cambodia will start to feel like a second home.

12.4 Benefits and Challenges Specific to Cambodia

Like any country, Cambodia presents its unique mix of advantages and challenges to expats. Understanding these can help you make the most of your time in this fascinating country:

Benefits:
- **Cost of Living**: Compared to many Western countries, Cambodia has a significantly lower cost of living. This makes it an attractive destination for expats seeking a more affordable lifestyle.
- **Cultural Experiences**: Cambodia offers a rich cultural heritage, evident in its ancient temples, traditional music, dance, and art. Living in Cambodia allows for a deep dive into this unique culture.
- **Natural Beauty**: From its pristine beaches and islands to lush jungles and the famous Angkor Wat temple complex, Cambodia is a haven for nature and history enthusiasts.
- **Growing Expat Community**: The country's growing expat community provides a supportive network for newcomers.

Challenges:

- **Language Barrier**: While English is spoken in many tourist areas and by younger generations, it is not widely spoken throughout the country. This can pose a challenge, but learning basic Khmer phrases can greatly help in daily life.

- **Infrastructure**: Depending on where you live, infrastructure might not be up to the standards you are used to. Roads can be poor, and power outages occur.
- **Healthcare**: While healthcare facilities are improving in larger cities like Phnom Penh, they can be subpar in more rural areas. Many expats choose to have health insurance that covers medical evacuation in emergencies.
- **Climate**: The tropical climate can take some getting used to, especially the hot and humid wet season.

Adapting to life in Cambodia can be a process, but by acknowledging and understanding these challenges, expats can equip themselves to navigate these hurdles and truly enjoy the many benefits that life in Cambodia offers.

12.5 Cambodian Society's Perception of Expats

The perception of expats in Cambodia can vary greatly depending on individual interactions, behaviors, and cultural awareness. Here are some general insights:

Respect for Foreigners: Cambodians are known for their warmth and hospitality towards foreigners, including expats. This respect often stems from an understanding that expats contribute to the local economy and can bring diverse skills and knowledge.

Value of Cultural Respect: Expats who show respect and interest towards Cambodian culture, traditions, and customs are typically well-regarded. This includes learning basic phrases in Khmer, dressing modestly, particularly at religious sites, and showing deference to local customs and social rules.

Impact of Behavior: Like anywhere in the world, the behavior of individual expats can shape perceptions. Those who behave respectfully and abide by local laws and regulations are more likely to be well-received. Conversely, disrespectful or disruptive behavior can create a negative impression.

Urban-Rural Divide: In cities with a high concentration of expats, such as Phnom Penh and Siem Reap, locals are more accustomed to interacting with foreigners. In more rural or remote areas, expats may be a less common sight, and reactions can vary.

In conclusion, the key to positive experiences and perceptions in Cambodia, as an expat, lies in demonstrating respect for the local culture, traditions, and laws, along with active efforts to integrate into the local community.

13. Planning the Move

13.1 Timeline and Checklist

Moving to a new country requires careful planning. Below is a general timeline and checklist for planning your move to Cambodia. Keep in mind that everyone's situation is unique, so adjust as needed.

Six Months Before the Move:

Research: Start by learning as much as you can about life in Cambodia, including culture, cost of living, healthcare, and legalities. Books, blogs, forums, and this guide are excellent resources.

Visas and Legalities: Determine which type of visa you'll need and start the application process. Consult with an immigration lawyer if necessary.

Three Months Before the Move:

Health Check-ups: Schedule medical, dental, and eye check-ups. Make sure you're up to date on vaccinations and understand the healthcare system in Cambodia.

Finances: Notify your bank of your move and explore banking options in Cambodia.

Housing: Start looking for housing, or at least decide on the area where you'd like to live.

One Month Before the Move:

Utilities and Subscriptions: Cancel or update your address for utilities, subscriptions, and mail.

Packing: Begin packing non-essential items. Decide what you'll ship, what you'll carry with you, and what you'll leave behind.

Pets: If you're bringing pets, ensure all their vaccinations are up-to-date and explore the pet importation process.

Final Weeks:

Farewells: Say goodbye to friends and family. Plan for ways to stay in touch.

Essential Documents: Gather all essential documents such as passport, visa, birth certificate, medical records, and insurance documents.

Final Days:

Double-check: Ensure all tasks are completed. Double-check flight details, accommodation, and transportation upon arrival in Cambodia.

Arrival in Cambodia:

Local Registration: Depending on your visa, you may need to register your arrival with local authorities.

Remember, moving abroad is a significant life event and can be stressful. But with proper planning and organization, you can ensure a smoother transition to your new life in Cambodia.

13.2 What to Bring

Deciding what to bring when you move to Cambodia can be a daunting task. Below are some general suggestions, but always consider your individual needs and lifestyle.

Clothing: Due to Cambodia's tropical climate, lightweight and breathable clothing is recommended. Don't forget modest attire for visiting religious sites. Even in the warmest months, it's a good idea to have a light sweater or jacket for air-conditioned environments.

Medication: If you take specific medication, it's advised to bring a sufficient supply until you can ensure its availability in Cambodia. Always carry a copy of your prescription.

Personal Care Products: While most personal care products are readily available, if you have specific brands or products you can't live without, it may be worth bringing a supply.

Electronics: Tech gadgets are typically more expensive in Cambodia. It's often beneficial to bring items such as laptops, smartphones, cameras, or tablets from home. Remember to pack the appropriate power adapters.

Books: English books can be hard to find outside of major cities. If you're an avid reader, consider bringing some books along or investing in an e-reader.

Important Documents: Don't forget necessary documents like your passport, visa, international driver's license, birth certificate, medical records, and copies of your prescriptions.

Spices and Specialty Food Items: While Cambodia has a diverse and delicious food culture, there might be some specific food items or spices from home that you'll miss and which might not be easily available.

Remember, it's important to balance between what you need and the cost and logistics of shipping. Furthermore, customs regulations may apply to certain items. Be sure to check the Cambodian customs regulations before packing.

13.3 Hiring a Moving Company

Hiring a reliable international moving company can make your transition to Cambodia much smoother. Here are some things to consider:

Experience with Cambodia: Look for a moving company that has experience with international moves, specifically to Cambodia. They'll be familiar with the logistics, customs regulations, and any potential challenges.

Services Offered: Some companies provide a comprehensive service that includes packing, shipping, and unpacking, while others may offer more basic services. Determine what level of service you require.

Insurance: Ensure the moving company offers adequate insurance coverage for your belongings during transit. Understanding the details of the insurance policy (what is covered, exclusions, claim process, etc.) is crucial.

Estimates: Obtain estimates from multiple companies. Be sure these estimates include all potential charges so you can accurately compare costs.

Customer Reviews: Check online reviews and ratings. Reach out to past customers if possible.

International Associations: Consider companies that are part of international moving associations, such as the International Association of Movers (IAM), which have standards their members must adhere to.

Once you've selected a moving company, stay in regular communication with them throughout the process. Make sure you understand the timeline, the documentation required, and the process once your belongings arrive in Cambodia.

13.4 Banking Considerations

Ensuring access to your finances is a critical aspect of your move to Cambodia. Here's what you need to consider:
Home Country Bank: Inform your current bank about your plans to move abroad to avoid any unexpected account freezes due to 'suspicious foreign activity'. Discuss the potential fees for overseas transactions and withdrawals. Some banks have partnerships with foreign banks, which can reduce or eliminate these fees.

Opening a Bank Account in Cambodia: While it's possible to get by in Cambodia using just cash and international cards, having a local bank account can make things easier, especially for receiving a salary if you plan to work. Explore the requirements for opening a bank account in Cambodia as a foreigner, which can often be done with your passport and a valid visa.

Online Banking: Online banking is a boon for expats. It allows you to manage your finances, pay bills, and transfer money from anywhere. Ensure your home bank provides a robust online banking system and see if your chosen Cambodian bank offers the same.

Currency: The official currency of Cambodia is the Riel, but the US Dollar is widely used. Understand the exchange rate and when each currency is typically used.

International Money Transfers: There may be times when you need to transfer money between your home country and Cambodia. Familiarize yourself with services like SWIFT transfers, or digital platforms like PayPal, Wise, or Revolut.

Emergency Access: Have a plan in place in case of a financial emergency. This could be a credit card that's accepted internationally, an agreement with your home bank, or a trusted individual who can send you money if needed. Before making any financial decisions, it's advisable to consult with a financial advisor who is familiar with expatriate finances.

13.5 Customs Regulations

Understanding customs regulations is crucial when moving to Cambodia. Here are some key considerations:

Restricted and Prohibited Items: Familiarize yourself with the list of restricted and prohibited items for importation into Cambodia. This includes firearms, narcotics, certain types of medications, and cultural artifacts. Ensure you comply with these regulations to avoid legal issues.

Duty and Taxes: Cambodia imposes customs duties and taxes on certain imported goods. The rates can vary depending on the type of item and its declared value. Research the duty and tax rates to understand the potential costs associated with importing your belongings.

Customs Declarations: When entering Cambodia, you'll need to complete a customs declaration form. Declare all items accurately and truthfully to avoid any complications.

Documents and Paperwork: Prepare the necessary documents for customs clearance, including your passport, visa, packing list, and inventory of your belongings. Ensure these documents are easily accessible and organized.

Temporary Importation: If you plan to bring certain items temporarily, such as electronics or personal belongings, for personal use, you may be able to declare them as temporary imports. This allows you to avoid paying customs duties and taxes, provided you can prove the items will be exported when you leave the country.

Professional Assistance: Consider hiring a customs broker or a moving company with experience in customs clearance procedures. They can guide you through the process, assist with paperwork, and ensure compliance with regulations. It's essential to stay up to date with the latest customs regulations, as they can change. Check with the Cambodian Customs and Excise Department or consult with a professional to ensure a smooth and compliant customs clearance process.

13.6 Notifying Home Country Government Agencies

Before your move to Cambodia, it's important to notify relevant government agencies in your home country. Here are some key agencies you may need to inform:

Tax Authorities: Contact the tax authority in your home country to update your residential status and understand your tax obligations as an expat living in Cambodia. They can provide guidance on filing requirements, any tax treaties between your home country and Cambodia, and potential tax implications.

Social Security or Pension Office: If you receive social security benefits or have a pension, inform the relevant office about your change of residence. This ensures that your benefits continue to be paid correctly and can prevent any disruptions.

Health Insurance Provider: If you have health insurance coverage in your home country, inform your provider about your move to Cambodia. Inquire about the coverage options available while living abroad and make any necessary adjustments to your policy.

Driver's License Authority: Check the requirements for maintaining or transferring your driver's license while living in Cambodia. Some countries may require you to obtain an international driver's license or provide a certified translation of your existing license.

Voter Registration: If you are a registered voter in your home country, determine if you need to update your voter registration status due to your change of residence. This may include updating your address or exploring absentee voting options.

Bank and Financial Institutions: Notify your bank and other financial institutions about your move to Cambodia. Update your contact information and discuss any necessary arrangements, such as international banking services or transferring funds.

Home Insurance Provider: If you own property in your home country, inform your home insurance provider about your change of residence. They can advise you on coverage options and any policy changes required.

Employer or Social Welfare Office: If you're employed or receive social welfare benefits, notify your employer or the relevant office about your relocation. Ensure that any necessary paperwork or changes to your benefits are completed.

Remember, specific requirements and processes may vary depending on your home country. It's recommended to contact these agencies well in advance of your move to Cambodia to ensure a smooth transition and to comply with any necessary obligations.

13.7 Relocation Services and Their Benefits

Relocating to a new country like Cambodia can be complex and overwhelming. Consider utilizing the services of relocation companies to simplify the process. Here are some benefits of using relocation services:

Expertise and Local Knowledge: Relocation companies specialize in helping individuals and families move to new countries. They have extensive knowledge of the local regulations, processes, and cultural nuances of Cambodia. Their expertise can guide you through the entire relocation journey, from visa applications to finding housing.

Orientation and Settling-In Assistance: Relocation companies often provide orientation programs to help you acclimate to your new surroundings. They can offer information on local neighborhoods, schools, healthcare facilities, transportation, and more. They may also assist with tasks like setting up utilities, obtaining local identification cards, or connecting with essential services.

Housing Search and Assistance: Finding suitable accommodation in a foreign country can be challenging. Relocation companies can help you identify housing options that meet your needs and budget. They can also facilitate property viewing, lease negotiations, and provide guidance on local rental laws and regulations.

School Search and Enrollment: If you have children, relocation services can assist in finding suitable schools and guide you through the enrollment process. They can provide information on international schools, local educational institutions, and help you navigate admission requirements.

Immigration and Visa Support: Relocation companies can assist with visa applications, work permits, and other immigration-related processes. They can guide you through the required documentation, submission procedures, and any changes in immigration policies.

Logistics and Moving Services: Relocation companies can handle the logistics of your move, including packing, shipping, and customs clearance. They have the experience and network to ensure a smooth transportation process for your belongings.

Ongoing Support: Even after you've settled into your new life in Cambodia, relocation companies often provide ongoing support. They can be a resource for any questions or concerns that may arise during your time as an expat.

While utilizing relocation services comes at a cost, the convenience, timesaving, and peace of mind they provide can make your transition to Cambodia much smoother. Consider weighing the benefits against your budget and specific needs to determine if relocation services are right for you.

Printed in Great Britain
by Amazon

40759864R00069